KAREN COUMBE MRCVS & KAREN BUSH

THE COMPLETE
EQUINE
EMERGENCY
BIBLE

THE COMPREHENSIVE GUIDE TO COPING WITH EVERY HORSE-RELATED EMERGENCY FROM FIRST AID TO ROAD SAFETY

Karen Bush: For Mick Wood – a constant inspiration

Karen Coumbe: To Polly and Florence,
without whose help this book could have been done in half the time!

Karen Bush holds the BHS Intermediate Teaching qualification, and for many years worked in commercial ABRS and BHS-approved riding establishments, teaching clients of all ages and levels.

Karen Coumbe BEVC, is a qualified veterinary surgeon and partner at the Bell Equine Veterinary Clinic, a Royal College of Veterinary Surgeons approved equine hospital in Mereworth, Kent. She has written several equine books and is veterinary correspondent for *Horse & Hound*. She is married with two daughters.

UK/US TERMINOLOGY

UK	US
Bandage	Wrap
Elastoplast®	Elastikon®
Cotton wool	Cotton
Epsom Salts	Magnesium Sulfate
Gamgee	Sheet cotton or combiroll
Headcollar	Halter
K Band	Brown gauze
Leadrope	Leadshank
Liquid paraffin	Mineral oil
Melonin®	Telfa pad
Nappies	Diapers
Pevidine	Betadine
Poultice	sometimes called sweat
Vaseline®	Petroleum jelly
Box	Stable or stall
Torch	Flashlight

A DAVID & CHARLES BOOK
Copyright © David & Charles Limited 2004, 2007

David & Charles is an F+W Publications Inc. company
4700 East Galbraith Road
Cincinnati, OH 45236

First published in the UK in 2004
Reprinted 2005
First US paperback edition 2006
Reprinted 2006

Copyright © Karen Coumbe & Karen Bush 2004, 2007

A catalogue record for this book is available from the British Library.

ISBN-13: 978-0-7153-1695-5 hardback
ISBN-10: 0-7153-1695-8 hardback

ISBN-13: 978-0-7153-2671-8 paperback
ISBN-10: 0-7153-2671-6 paperback

Printed in Singapore by KHL Printing Co Ltd
for David & Charles
Brunel House   Newton Abbot   Devon

Commissioning Editor Jane Trollope
Desk Editor Sarah Martin
Art Editor Sue Cleave
Copy Editor Anne Plume
Production Controller Jennifer Campbell

Visit our website at www.davidandcharles.co.uk

David & Charles books are available from all good bookshops; alternatively you can contact our Orderline on 0870 9908222 or write to us at FREEPOST EX2 110, D&C Direct, Newton Abbot, TQ12 4ZZ (no stamp required UK only); US customers call 800-289-0963 and Canadian customers call 800-840-5220.

Contents

Genuine accidents can and do happen; they can rarely be predicted, and on the odd occasion that you can see a problem about to happen, it is often too late to do anything about it, other than cope with the consequences. Bear in mind that many accidents can generally be prevented with a modicum of common sense, good observation, and a bit of forethought: there really is no excuse for either an accident or an emergency arising as a result of negligence, laziness or sloppy habits.

'Fail to Plan, Plan to Fail'

A very useful motto to keep in mind! Forward planning can make dealing with emergencies considerably more efficient and much less stressful.

❑ Keep an adequately stocked first aid kit.

❑ Keep a list of vital phone numbers to hand: your vet; farrier; doctor; lorry rescue; horse's owner.

❑ Store your vet's number in your mobile phone (see also pp 102).

❑ At the stable yard keep a list of contact numbers displayed in a prominent position.

❑ Keep your insurance documents to hand.

It is easy to become complacent. Many of the accidents that occur around horses are with animals that are familiar to you and known to be generally placid in disposition in most matters. Those horses that are less predictable in their actions or behaviour usually command a healthy respect and greater care is taken in their management; but safe handling and riding practices should always be applied to all equines, regardless of temperament, if risks are to be minimized.

Should an emergency or an accident occur, it is important to consider the advice offered here only as a guide, since although some situations may be similar, no two are identical. Use logic and common sense, think before you act, and be prepared to be flexible, and to adapt what you do according to the demands of each individual incident.

Also, although suggestions as to future actions to take following an emergency may be made where appropriate, this book is not intended as a schooling, medical or remedial training manual: first-hand professional guidance should always be sought where a problem persists, and is potentially serious.

Veterinary Emergencies

It is now well recognized that if the initial treatment of any injury or illness is effective, it will help promote a rapid and successful recovery. The information provided in the veterinary section is there to indicate what is normal for the horse, then if there is any change from normal, to help with those crucial first stages in managing what could be a potential crisis. **It is not intended to circumvent or replace regular veterinary care,** and should not be used as such; rather, the aim is to help you recognize when a horse has a problem, and to devise an action plan to cope.

The contents of Part 1 should help answer many of the questions frequently

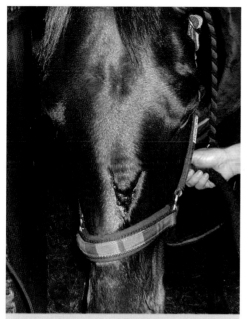

Do not panic: many injuries look worse than they really are when first viewed. This head wound healed well after being stitched

put to equine vets. The intention is not to stop you talking to your own vet, but rather, to help you decide when you might need to contact them. It is important to establish good communications with your vet; thus, it is unreasonable to ring them at midnight for a horse that has already been ill for three days, but it is also unfair to leave a sick horse to the following day if he requires urgent treatment. There is a fine balance to be struck here, which needs good judgement, experience, and some intuition! Basically, it is always better to ring to ask for advice rather than leave a horse untreated, at the risk of making things worse at a later stage.

By discussing any concerns you might have with your vet, an apparent crisis may

Emergency Procedure

If you are present in any emergency situation observe the following procedure:

❑ **Remain Calm**
Easier said than done, but remember that you will be dealing with a horse and/or rider who may well be panicking. An air of confidence and control can help to reassure both and possibly prevent further damage.

❑ Alert any professional services that may be needed as soon as possible.

❑ Enlist assistance wherever possible; even relatively minor emergencies may need more than one pair of hands.

❑ Do no more than you can accomplish without compromising your own safety or that of others. Bear in mind the potential for injury to those assisting you by a horse that is frightened or in pain: the preservation of human life must always take precedence over that of equines.

❑ Wear appropriate protective clothing, eg sturdy footwear.

❑ After the incident, notify all relevant parties such as relatives, the horse's owner, insurance companies.

Are these horses just resting, or is there something wrong? In fact they are just sunbathing, but it is a good example of why it is essential for us to get used to observing what is normal for our animals

be resolved with some simple advice. On the other hand, if you do have a major emergency and a vet knows you and your horses, they will be more likely to respond promptly to your cry for help. Vets usually work in relatively small private practices, with only a limited number of experienced individuals sharing the equine on-call duties. Furthermore, all vets are required to provide a 24-hour emergency service, so be aware that the vet you disturb at night will probably have to work the following day; therefore try to avoid unnecessary night-time calls. It is also very frustrating for them to be contacted late at night about a horse that would have been far better seen the previous morning. By recognizing potential emergencies early on, your horse can have more rapid and effective veterinary care, meaning less worry and expense for you.

First Aid for People

Part 3 deals with first aid for humans. The aims are the same as those for horses:
- ❏ to preserve life;
- ❏ to prevent any worsening of the condition;
- ❏ to promote the casualty's recovery.

Many falls result in nothing worse than a few bruises, but they can sometimes be more serious; injuries can also occur when handling as well as riding horses, and around the stableyard whilst carrying out chores. If you are with someone who sustains injury, it may be down to you to give first aid. Bear in mind that this is not intended to be a comprehensive guide to human first aid, and that it is well worth taking a first aid training course of some kind.

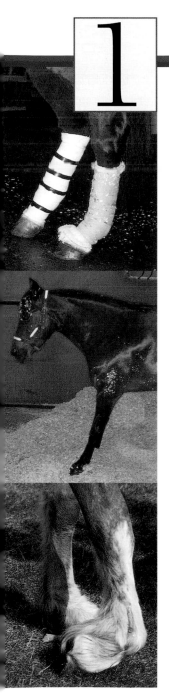

1 Veterinary Care in Emergencies

In this section

What is First Aid?

First aid is the initial help that is given following injury or illness. It may need to be followed up by 'second aid', which could involve more sophisticated treatment or investigations, depending on the severity of the initial problem. The objectives of first aid are to:

❏ preserve life;
❏ prevent suffering;
❏ stabilize the patient's (human or equine) condition;
❏ relieve acute conditions;
❏ promote recovery.

The Rules of First Aid

DO NOT PANIC

A calm, sensible approach will reassure the horse and benefit all concerned. When you discover something is wrong, take a deep breath and make an action plan. Equine veterinary nurses are taught to make a rapid assessment, and then to act on it. The more urgent the situation, the less evaluation is needed, and the more immediately action needs to be taken. Follow the sequence of steps described here:

S Scan: rapidly evaluate the people, the horse, and the environment.

I Identify: the relevant problems, and predict the most likely results.

P Prioritize: decide where the immediate needs lie.

P Plan: what action should be taken, and by whom.

E Execute: the plan.

R Reassess: repeat, and continue until the horse and people involved are stabilized.

ENSURE THE SAFETY OF ALL

❏ A distressed horse can behave unpredictably, so always ensure the safety of all present.
❏ If practical, seek help before doing anything drastic yourself, and **never** put yourself at risk, as the situation will only be made worse if you are hurt as well as your horse!

❏ If you are first on the scene, secure the horse, ideally by putting on a headcollar (which is a good reason for always carrying one in your car), and try to reassure them; then stop, think calmly and logically, and summon help.

CONTACT YOUR VET

With modern methods of communication such as mobile phones, pagers and the like, it should be relatively easy to contact your vet to ask if your problem really is an emergency. It is important to observe the following procedure:

❏ Always explain when you ring that you think you have a possible emergency.
❏ Have ready all the necessary information: the horse's name and the owner's details, the location, and your phone number so you can be rung back.

❑ Ensure you keep the line free, so the vet can ring you straight back; do not ring anyone else until you have talked to the vet.

❑ The best person to talk to the vet is the one who knows most about the horse's illness or injury.

❑ If a horse is seriously ill or injured it may be necessary to transport him to a clinic, where better facilities are available for treatment.

❑ It will always be better for a horse to travel sooner rather than later, whilst he is still fit to do so; no one will complain if he has recovered by the time he arrives. And if he takes a turn for the worse and has already been taken to an equine hospital, then he is certainly in the right place. Obviously if your horse is kept a long way from a specialist equine hospital facility, or if he is unfit to travel, then you and your vet may have to manage more major problems at home.

WHEN TO CALL THE VET

With all potential emergencies, experience helps in recognizing a true crisis. If in doubt, call your vet for help or advice.

If your horse suffers a major injury, develops severe colic, or is otherwise clearly in acute pain, obviously you need to contact your vet straightaway. There are also some problems, in particular apparently minor injuries, that some owners dismiss as unimportant initially, but which would benefit from urgent veterinary attention. In between are a host of conditions that can cause varying degrees of concern, and also varying degrees of uncertainty as to whether or not a visit from the vet is justified. It is impossible to describe every situation or to provide set rules for each one; however, conditions where there would be cause for concern include colic, lameness, wounds, choke and foaling.

❑ Colic
Delay may be dangerous.
No matter how experienced you are, if even a mild colic persists for more than half an hour, or if a colic subsides but then recurs, you should at least speak to your vet.

❑ Lameness
May require urgent treatment.
In general, if a horse is standing on only three legs and cannot walk, you should contact your vet straightaway. If, on the other hand, a horse can walk on the lame leg but prefers to rest it, it is less critical, but would still be best seen by a vet (or the farrier if the problem is shoeing related) the same day.

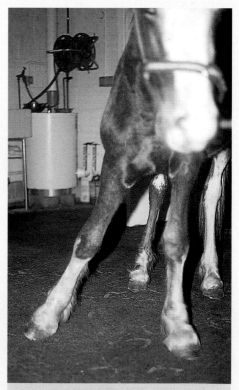

Abnormal leg position observed in a pony with a fracture to the right foreleg

❑ Wounds

The wound's position is crucial.

Wounds often cause confusion. Any fresh, clean cut that has gone right through the skin so that the sides gape apart is a possible candidate for stitching. Usually it is only worthwhile stitching a wound if it is fresh (less than 6 to 8 hours old). Many wounds will heal very well without being stitched at all. However, any wound near a joint or other vital structure – for example, the tendon sheath at the back of the pastern – must be taken seriously, as such damage can permanently cripple a horse. You should contact your vet at once if you notice any such injury, particularly if there appears to be only a small puncture wound, but it is causing a more severe lameness than one would expect.

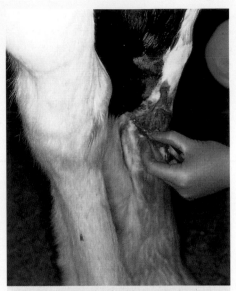

A wound being checked by a vet

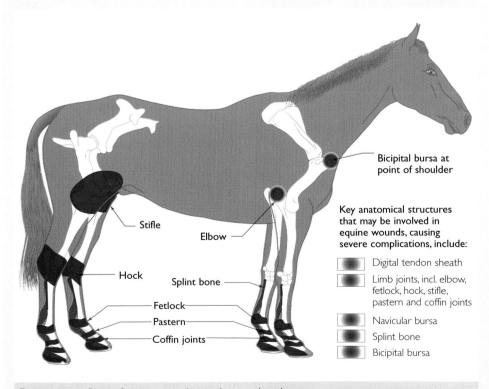

Bicipital bursa at point of shoulder

Stifle

Elbow

Hock

Splint bone

Fetlock

Pastern

Coffin joints

Key anatomical structures that may be involved in equine wounds, causing severe complications, include:

- Digital tendon sheath
- Limb joints, incl. elbow, fetlock, hock, stifle, pastern and coffin joints
- Navicular bursa
- Splint bone
- Bicipital bursa

Danger areas: Sites of some wounds worth worrying about

❑ Choke

Generally has the appearance of a dire emergency, but is usually less serious than it seems; the majority of cases will clear themselves before your vet arrives. Choke occurs when food gets stuck in a horse's throat. The important thing is to prevent the horse from eating or drinking anything further: put him in a box with no hay and non-edible bedding, then contact your vet for advice. Very often by the time you have finished the phone call, the obstruction will have cleared. However, although it is not always the emergency that it first appears, if the obstruction does not shift within an hour, you will need help from your vet.

❑ Foaling difficulties

The number one red-alert emergency. Once something goes wrong, every minute is vital if mare and foal are to survive. It is best that a mare should foal down where there is experienced help to hand; alternatively you should contact your vet as soon as foaling starts.

Colicing foal

REASSURE YOUR HORSE

Whilst you are waiting for the vet to arrive, do what you can to comfort the horse. There are specific things you can do to help certain conditions, which can be found in the relevant sections; however, **the golden rule to remember above all others is to do no harm.** How much you can safely and legally do depends on the condition with which you are coping. For instance, if you have a wound that is bleeding badly, you need to apply a pressure pad to staunch the blood flow, rather than wait for the vet to arrive and do it for you. Use your common sense: for instance, most lame horses are best brought in from the field; however, if a horse has a suspected broken leg, it is unreasonable to distress him further by trying to make him walk.

The Horse's Vital Signs

If you know what is normal for a horse, you will be quicker to recognize when something is wrong. Careful daily observation is the best way of picking up subtle changes that may indicate that a horse is off colour, and a simple way to remember what to look for is to think of ABC, meaning Appearance, Behaviour, Condition. Check each of these in turn to monitor a horse's well-being. Thus a horse that seems just a bit dull and off his feed may have a sky-high temperature and need urgent treatment. If your horse feels hot, or cold, or is sweating, one of the first things you should do is to check his temperature so keep a thermometer handy.

	Normal rates
Temperature	37° to 38°C (Centigrade) or 100° to 101°F (Fahrenheit)
Pulse	32 to 42 beats per minute
Respiratory rate at rest	Between 8 to 14 breaths per minute

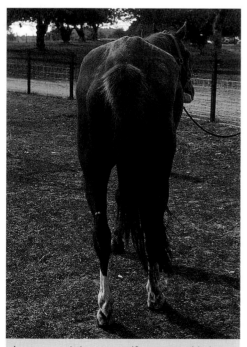

Appearance is important. If you see a thin horse every day you may fail to notice weight loss

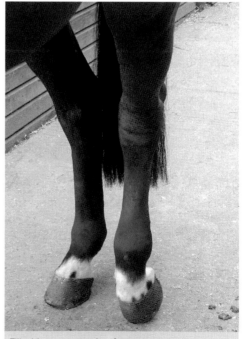

Filled leg as a result of a wound. A high temperature can be a sign of infection

Checking Your Horse's Temperature

How to take the temperature

❑ Grease the measuring end with some lubrication, such as petroleum jelly (Vaseline®) or saliva. For safety have someone reassuring the horse and steadying his head.

❑ A horse's temperature is taken in the rectum. Stand to one side of the horse's rear; run your hand over the quarters and then grasp the base of the tail firmly.

❑ Lift the tail and then insert the bulb end of the thermometer into the anus. Keep hold of the tail so the horse does not clamp it down, but also hang on to the thermometer.

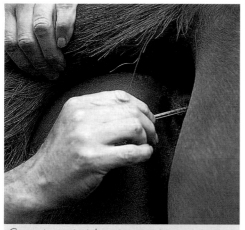

Correct way to take a temperature

❑ Remain at the side of the horse to avoid being kicked. Leave the thermometer inserted for about a minute. Make sure you tilt it against the wall of the rectum.

❑ Gently remove the thermometer, wipe it clean with cotton wool or a tissue, and read it. Afterwards clean it with cold water and disinfectant.

❑ If the horse's temperature is high or low, always check it 30 minutes later in order to confirm the reading.

Slightly increased temperature

Not usually serious, and normal after exercise.

High temperature, over 40°C or 102.5°F

Potentially serious; it suggests that the horse is ill, with a viral or bacterial infection, or is in pain.

Very low temperature

Suggests the horse is not well, and may be in a state of shock.

Using a Thermometer

Special veterinary thermometers can be purchased, although a human thermometer will work. The ideal is an easy-to-read digital thermometer.

If you use a glass thermometer, make sure the mercury is shaken right down to its bulb end before you start, as it will not record a lower reading accurately if the mercury is at the top of the scale.

Some identification microchips will also tell the horse's temperature, when the special reader device is used.

Although temperature is usually recorded in degrees Centigrade (°C), some people are more familiar with the use of Fahrenheit (°F) values. Whilst most thermometers show temperature on both scales, some do not. For conversion, the following equations should be used:

$$°C = (°F-32) \times 5/9$$
$$°F = (°C \times 9/5) + 32$$

Checking the Pulse and Heart Rate

Being able to check your horse's pulse and heart rate will help you monitor his well-being. The heart rate at rest will vary from one individual animal to another, depending as it does on a variety of factors, such as age, breed and degree of fitness. The horse's heart is a large, efficient pump so only needs to pump relatively slowly – and in fact it will occasionally miss a beat at rest, which is perfectly normal, but disconcerting when you are trying to measure the rate. Practise finding your horse's pulse after they have been working, when it will be stronger and therefore more obvious.

How to feel the heartbeat

The heartbeat in the horse is most easily felt on the left side of the lower chest where the girth would go just behind the elbow. The pulse is the actual pressure beat as the blood is rhythmically pumped through the arteries. The heart rate and pulse rate are usually the same.

Taking the horse's pulse

The horse's resting pulse is slow, so can be difficult to detect.

- ❑ The best place to feel it is where the facial artery passes under the jaw. Make sure the head is still and the horse is not eating.
- ❑ Run your fingers along the bony lower edge

of the jaw; the pulsing artery will be felt as a tubular structure.

- ❑ If you lightly press this against the jaw with the flat of your first two or three fingers, you will feel the pulse.
- ❑ Count the number of beats in 15 seconds, and multiply by four to get the pulse rate per minute.

Other Pulse Points

Other good places that you can feel the pulse, particularly in the headshy horse, are:

- ❑ inside the forelimb just below the elbow on what is called the axillary artery;
- ❑ at the back of the fetlock, where the digital artery runs down to the foot (this pulse will pound if a horse or pony has laminitis or pus in the foot, because there will be blood rushing to the foot);
- ❑ the tail under the dock, a good place for feeling the coccygeal artery in a horse that does not kick.

Raised pulse rate

First consider the following reasons for an unexpectedly high rate:

- ❑ If he is nervous or alarmed, for example when a vet or other stranger approaches him, then his pulse will shoot up. But when he calms down, his pulse will quickly return to normal too. Anxiety is a common reason for a transient increase in pulse rate.
- ❑ Exercise: if a horse has just been worked, his pulse will be faster than normal. The pulse rate depends on the amount of exercise given, the period of recovery time, and how fit the horse is.
- ❑ If your horse is injured whilst competing, do not be alarmed if the pulse is fast when it is first measured. Always allow time for a pulse to return to normal.

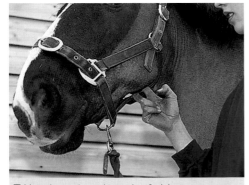

Taking the pulse where the facial artery passes under the jaw

Persistently raised pulse rate

Reasons for a persistently raised pulse include:

- ❏ pain;
- ❏ fever;
- ❏ heat exhaustion;
- ❏ shock;
- ❏ heart disease.

If your horse consistently has a very fast pulse – over 80 beats per minute – there is something serious going on. You should look for other signs, such as colic, and contact your vet.

Low pulse rate

A low pulse usually indicates a relaxed, fit and hopefully healthy horse; however, it can be associated with serious conditions such as shock, hypothermia, or even poisoning. If you have a low pulse and a healthy horse, do not worry; but if the horse looks ill, you should first take his temperature. If the horse is shocked, he will have a weak pulse, and you must try to find out why. If there is no obvious reason that you can rectify – for instance, by warming him up with rugs – then talk to your vet.

Checking the Respiratory Rate

The respiratory rate increases with exercise, pain and high temperatures, as well as respiratory disease itself. Any significant change should be taken seriously. A horse with a severe breathing problem will have only one heartbeat for three breaths, or even worse. When a horse has difficulty breathing the whole flank will heave up and down with the extra respiratory effort: hence the name 'heaves' for a severe stable cough and dust allergy.

How to measure the respiratory rate

The best way to measure this is to either hold a hand close to the horse's nostrils to feel each breath, or to count the flank movements as the horse breathes in and out. On a cold day you will be able to see each time he exhales. It is worth noting that a horse usually has around three heartbeats to every one breath, and this ratio stays about the same with exercise, although not with disease.

What Else to Check?

Appetite

You should know what an individual horse eats. For many, being off their food is a crucial clue that they are unwell. Some fit animals are fussy and will go off their feed for no reason, but most ponies and some horses are stomachs on legs, and if they stop eating, something significant must be wrong.

Thirst

Horses normally drink 20 to 45 litres of water a day, but this varies with the weather, with their exercise levels, and the moisture in the rest of their diet.

Droppings

Loose droppings or diarrhoea are a cause for concern. Equally you should be worried if a horse has passed fewer droppings than he does normally, as this may lead to constipation (known as impaction) or to colic.

Most healthy horses are keen to eat

Tell-tale curly coat of a case of Cushing's Disease; commonly seen in older animals

Urine

A horse's urine can normally be very cloudy, and can range in colour from pale yellow to brown. You should be concerned if it appears red, or if the horse is repeatedly straining to pass urine.

Skin

This should be supple, and there should be a shine to the coat.

Mucous membranes

The membranes around the eye and on the gums should be a healthy salmon-pink colour (except for the occasional horse that has pigmented gums). Check the circulation by measuring the 'capillary refill time': to do this, press a pink area of the gums; it will blanche under the pressure, then when you take the pressure away, it should return to its normal pink colour within 3 seconds. A delay suggests a circulatory problem such as shock.

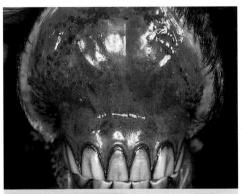

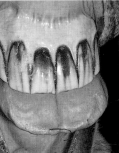

Above: Unhealthy membranes with bleeding as well as normal black pigmentation

Pale membranes around the gums and lips suggesting anaemia

Sweating

If this is not linked to exercise, it suggests that something is wrong. The horse may be in pain.

Mental state

A healthy horse should prick his ears and look interested in his surroundings. If he is dull and unresponsive, something may be wrong.

Lameness

Usually this means that one or more legs are painful, although sometimes there will be a mechanical lameness, where some restriction simply prevents a limb from bending properly. If a horse is very lame he will not be able to stand on the affected leg; subtle lameness is much harder to appreciate.

To test for lameness

❑ Ask someone to walk and then trot the horse away from you, and then back towards you on the end of a leadrope, with the head held loosely so you can watch him move.

❑ Lameness is most obvious at trot: in a horse that is lame in front the head will lift up as the lame leg hits the ground, and it will nod down as the sound leg hits the ground.

Non weight-bearing lameness. This pony cannot stand on the right fore, and hops along with two legs off the ground at once

❑ Hind-limb lameness can be harder to see, but is most obvious as a horse trots away from you. The hip on the painful lame side appears to rise and fall more obviously as the horse tries to avoid taking weight on that leg.

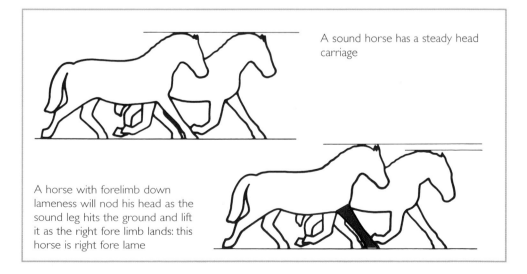

A sound horse has a steady head carriage

A horse with forelimb down lameness will nod his head as the sound leg hits the ground and lift it as the right fore limb lands: this horse is right fore lame

The First Aid Kit

Basic Travelling Kit

1 Digital thermometer

2 A good antiseptic

Such as Hibiscrub® (chlorhexidine) or pevidine.

3 Moist wound gel

Can be plastered on a wound to protect and cleanse it, properly called a hydrogel. These are a far better option than the various wound powders or creams that are available. Suitable brands include:

❑ Vetalintex® hydrogel wound dressing made by Robinsons in small 25g tubes;

❑ Derma Gel® pump in big 100ml toothpaste tube-like dispensers manufactured by Maximilian Zenho & Co and marketed by Equine America;

❑ Various other makes appear on the market, such as Nu-gel® and IntraSite® gel.

4 Cotton wool

At least one roll, mainly for padding for dressings, and for moistening and cleaning wounds. If pushed for space you could use antiseptic wipes for wound cleaning.

5 Dressings and bandage materials

It would be advisable to include the following items:

❑ Non-stick dressings to go over wounds, such as Melonin® or Rondopad®; these come in a variety of sizes;

❑ Stretchable conforming bandages such as Vetrap®, or the cheaper gauze type that can be taped, such as Kband®;

❑ Sticky bandage such as Elastoplast®; a cheaper alternative is 5cm- or 10cm-wide duct tape, and 1cm-wide sticky tape to tape bandages in place;

❑ Gamgee, a square of which makes a useful pressure pad;

❑ Animalintex® poultice dressing;

❑ Padding to go around a limb between the non-stick dressing and the bandage. Cotton wool works well, gamgee is another option.

6 Curved scissors

7 Pocket torch

8 Chemical coolpack

A useful travelling first aid option to use as a cold compress. There are many that are specifically designed for applying to equine tendons, and others that are primarily for human use.

9 Clean bucket or bowl

To fill with dilute antiseptic to wash wounds.

10 Hoofpick

For the classic occasion when a stone becomes stuck in a foot.

In addition: A list of important telephone numbers, plus pen and paper for notes, and your insurance details, are all useful in a crisis.

Take a Spare

Always travel with a spare headcollar or halter (ideally an adjustable rope one that fits all sizes) and leadrope in case you come across a loose horse (see p123).

Additional Items for Most Emergencies

11 Tweezers
For picking out thorns and splinters.

12 A big torch

13 Many more bandages
On the basis that they are always useful.

14 Pliers and wire cutters
For the horse that gets tangled up in a fence.

15 Sterile antiseptic impregnated brushes
To clean wounds, such as E-Z Scrub®, an antiseptic-impregnated scrubbing brush.

16 Clean towels or rolls of paper towel

17 Baler twine and thick rope

18 Petroleum jelly
Useful to lubricate the thermometer; also to apply to the hindquarters to prevent the skin being scalded by diarrhoea, or to the skin below a discharging wound.

19 Shoe-removing kit
For emergency use only; otherwise the farrier should be contacted.

20 Disposable nappies
Clean disposable nappies (diapers) to use as foot bandages: the hoof is similar in size to a baby's bottom, which means that a nappy can be quickly taped on as protection in an emergency.

There are many other useful items that can be added to this list; however, if everyone always had everything on this list in clean, up-to-date condition, they could cope with most emergencies. It is worth considering **special feeds, such as bran** for a bran mash, either for a colic case or for a fit animal suddenly on enforced box rest. Similarly **common salt** and **Epsom salts** are sometimes used as emergency feed additives. The salt can also be used to make a saline wash if no antiseptic is available. Also include a few **sachets of decent disinfectant** in case

Replace Used Kit
Remember to replace any items you have used, and to add anything else you wished you had had when you did experience an emergency!

you need to disinfect an area or set up a foot dip if you have to suddenly isolate an infectious case.

There is always a temptation to include medication such as standard painkillers and antibiotics in a first aid box. However, it is far better to check with a vet at the time, rather than give the wrong thing.

Bandaging

It is essential to know when and how to use bandages, as they are a crucial part of first aid in the horse.

In an emergency, what a bandage looks like doesn't really matter; what is important is that it is not put on too tight and that it protects the injury. An overtight bandage may cause damage to skin and tissues, especially if it is left on for more than two hours. The horse may not show any signs of discomfort from an excessively tight bandage, so ensure that:

- ❑ the injured area is adequately protected;
- ❑ the bandage fits snugly and is well padded;
- ❑ pressure over the tendons is even;
- ❑ you are careful to avoid applying pressure over bony prominences such as the bone at the back of the knee and the point of the hock. These should be adequately padded, or the bandage split to avoid pressure sores;
- ❑ the opposite limb is supported when a horse is severely lame, especially in heavy individuals.

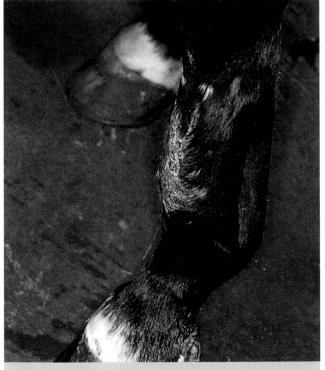

Healed pressure sore from carelessly applied bandages resulting in an ugly blemish

Functions of a Bandage:

- ❑ to cover wounds to control bleeding and swelling;
- ❑ to protect the injury from further trauma;
- ❑ to provide a clean environment for wound healing;
- ❑ to keep a dressing in place;
- ❑ to restrict movement and reduce pain.

Composition of a Bandage

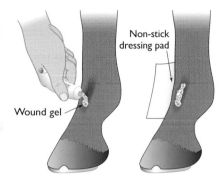

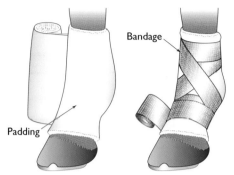

A bandage should consist of three layers, properly known as the primary, secondary and tertiary layers.

The primary layer

Usually this is a non-stick dressing pad – for example, Melonin® or Rondopad® – which may be held in place by soft cotton bandage padding such as Soffban®. For emergency treatment of a wound, apply a wound gel (hydrogel) to the damaged area, then the dressing pad will stick to that as you bandage over the top. There are many other dressings available to apply directly to wounds, but most are expensive and specialized. Your vet will tell you the dressings that will be required for a particular injury.

The secondary layer

This is the padding that protects the injury, absorbs discharges, and controls swelling. It is this second layer that is sometimes skimped or even forgotten, with potentially disastrous consequences. With inadequate padding and overtight bandaging, there is a risk of causing a so-called 'bandage bow' (localized swelling), a pressure sore, or even long-term scars that will cause permanent white hairs. A variety of padding materials can be used. Cotton wool is

cheap and works well, because it conforms very well to the shape of the horse's leg.

The tertiary layer

This secures the bandage and helps hold the dressing in place, as well as providing extra support and protection. Commonly some sort of stretch bandage is used that sticks to itself, such as Vetrap®, or a stretchy conforming bandage such as Kband®, together with adhesive tape or a sticky bandage such as Elastoplast®. Generally this sealing layer should not extend beyond the edge of the underlying padding in case it causes sores by rubbing; this is particularly true with foot bandages, where the heels and the back of the pastern are easily traumatized. On some other sites, however, such as the hock or knee, the only way to prevent a dressing slipping down may be to use a sticky bandage extending on to the skin.

An injured horse may well be excited, anxious, and perhaps even too dangerous to bandage without sedation; it may be all you can do to apply a pressure wrap to control bleeding. Do not struggle to put a big bandage on, since it will need to be removed by the vet when they arrive.

Practical Application

Hock bandages

Many horses resent their limbs being immobilized, especially the hock, and they will panic and kick out violently when they first try to move, which may be part way through the application of the bandage. The shape of the hock makes it difficult enough to bandage, even when the horse is not moving. Padding around the vulnerable areas at the front and back of the hock is important, as is the need to reduce tension over the point of the hock.

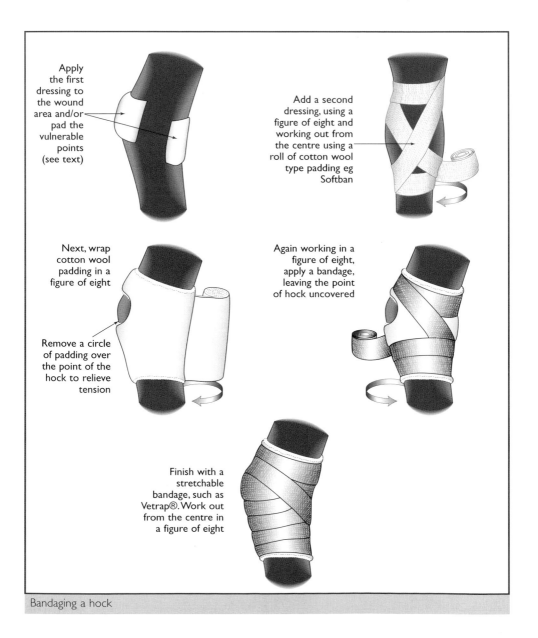

Apply the first dressing to the wound area and/or pad the vulnerable points (see text)

Add a second dressing, using a figure of eight and working out from the centre using a roll of cotton wool type padding eg Softban

Next, wrap cotton wool padding in a figure of eight

Remove a circle of padding over the point of the hock to relieve tension

Again working in a figure of eight, apply a bandage, leaving the point of hock uncovered

Finish with a stretchable bandage, such as Vetrap®. Work out from the centre in a figure of eight

Bandaging a hock

Hock and knee bandages

These have a tendency to fall down, which is best prevented by bandaging the lower limb as well to prevent slippage. If you have to bandage either of these areas repeatedly, a vet can supply elasticated stockings (known as Pressage® bandages) designed to fit either the hock or the knee, which will hold everything in place.

Apply the first dressing to the wound area

Apply a secondary dressing to hold the first in place using a roll of cotton wool type padding eg Softban

Continue in a figure of eight, avoiding the area over the carpal bone

Wrap cotton wool padding around the knee, removing a circle over the carpal bone to relieve tension

Next, apply a bandage in a figure of eight, working out from the centre

As before, avoid covering the area over the carpal bone. Leave a narrow band of padding visible above and below the bandage

Finish with a stretchable bandage, such as Vetrap®. Work out from the centre in a figure of eight.

Bandaging a knee

Foot bandages

This bandage is far simpler to apply, but because the horse will be walking on it all the time, inevitably it will get wet, and so it will need to be changed at least once a day. Using a nappy works well in an emergency, and then the whole area can be protected with sticky tape (see diagrams). If you are applying a foot poultice, this can be inserted inside the nappy. A square of aluminium foil over the poultice will help keep the heat in. Poultice boots are sometimes useful, especially for stabled horses or those that are difficult to bandage. Special hospital plate shoes can be fitted by a farrier for long-term foot dressings.

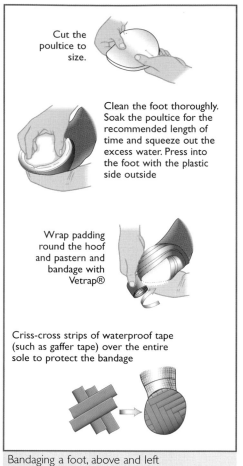

Cut the poultice to size.

Clean the foot thoroughly. Soak the poultice for the recommended length of time and squeeze out the excess water. Press into the foot with the plastic side outside

Wrap padding round the hoof and pastern and bandage with Vetrap®

Criss-cross strips of waterproof tape (such as gaffer tape) over the entire sole to protect the bandage

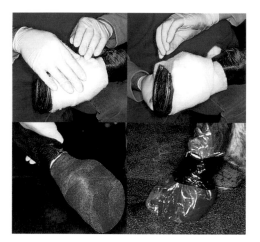

Bandaging a foot, above and left

Fetlock bandages

This joint is relatively easy to bandage, and you should proceed in the same way as a normal exercise bandage. Always provide plenty of padding, and watch for pressure sores at the front and back of the joint.

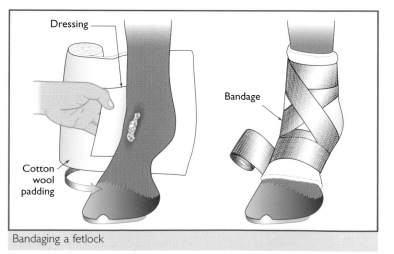

Dressing

Cotton wool padding

Bandage

Bandaging a fetlock

The Robert Jones bandage

This is a heavily padded limb bandage, made up of several compressed layers of cotton wool. It aims to provide strength, rigidity and even pressure, and to achieve:

- ❑ limb support;
- ❑ control of limb oedema;
- ❑ stabilization of fractures;
- ❑ protection of soft tissues.

A full-limb Robert Jones bandage (RJB) requires 8–10 rolls of cotton wool, and 15–20 conforming bandages. In the forelimb it usually extends from the floor to the point of the elbow, and in the hind limb from the floor to above the hock. The finished bandage should be an even tubular cylinder, and should sound like a ripe melon when tapped. It requires skill to apply, and should be left to a vet unless you want to waste a lot of dressings!

An RJB will provide support, but if a fracture is suspected, a splint will also need to be incorporated to increase the bandage's rigidity; ideally it should immobilize the joints above and below the area of damage. Many things can be improvised as splints in an emergency, such as a broom handle, wood (45 x 20mm), farriers' rasps, plastic piping or guttering (112mm diameter cut in half). Proper limb immobilization requires knowledge of limb anatomy and fractures, so is also a job for the vet.

A Robert Jones bandage requires skill and practice to apply properly. It is a job for your vet!

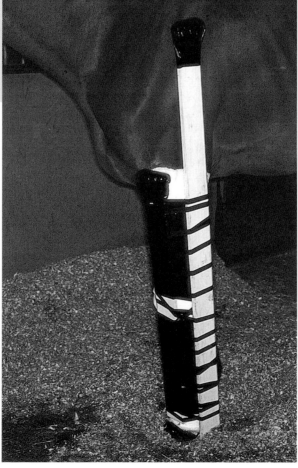

Box Rest

A horse may have to be confined to his box for a period of enforced rest as a part of convalescence for many conditions, most usually lameness, but it may also be when recovering after surgery. For instance, after colic surgery a horse's exercise routine will need to be severely restricted – box rest and walking in hand – for at least 4 weeks in most cases, in order to give the abdominal wound a chance to heal. After that they may be turned out into a small paddock for a further 4 to 8 weeks. Special care is needed in handling a horse on box rest.

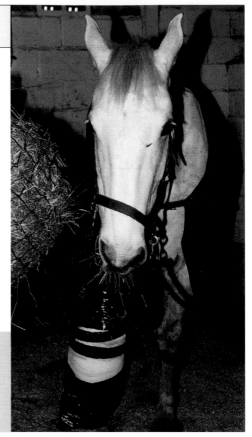

Horse recovering from a radial fracture after several weeks of box rest. This horse is cross-tied so he cannot lie down with miminal bedding so that he does not trip up. He has a big haynet with small holes to stave off boredom. Ideally the left fore should have a support bandage too

What to Watch For

When a horse is confined to their stable for any length of time, it is important to adapt your stable management routine to help them cope with the restrictions: they will get bored, they will need a revised feeding plan, their behaviour and temperament may change (for the worse), they will be more susceptible to physical complications such as colic. All these problems may be anticipated, and need to be addressed.

Boredom

Confinement may cause temperament problems: many equine orthopaedic patients will require prolonged periods of box rest, but they may not feel ill or in pain, and may become thoroughly frustrated. Horses that have suffered injury while competing are particularly difficult, as they will be fit and lively. Regular grooming will help, as will stable toys, a radio, and other horses or animals for company, such as chickens or sheep. The choice of stable can significantly affect a horse's stress levels; thus some are kept amused if they have a lot to watch, whilst others find this even more frustrating. Furthermore, stabled horses that have gone off their feed and are not eating are more likely to develop abnormal behaviour, previously called vices and now referred to as stereotypical behaviour, such as crib-biting, windsucking or weaving.

Feeding

It will be necessary to cut the horse's hard (corn) feed if he must be kept in and is not being exercised. Change to a high forage diet so that he has plenty to munch, as eating keeps a horse occupied. Hay or short-chop forages that take longer to eat are better than haylage. Splitting any concentrates into multiple small feeds will help.

Take care leading out

Always ensure that a horse is adequately restrained. Some that are normally fairly relaxed, may become difficult after being 'confined to barracks'. If there is any doubt as to his behaviour the horse should wear a bridle or Chifney bit, and the handler should wear gloves too.

Colic

This is a risk for horses that are confined to their stable. Frequent short walks to graze in hand will help, if permitted as part of the treatment regime. Several factors increase the risks of colic in box-resting horses; these include:

❑ Medical treatment, especially anaesthetics, as these will reduce gut motility.

❑ Pain also decreases gut motility, as does lack of exercise.

❑ A change in eating patterns, such as a reduced grass intake, will predispose a horse to impaction (constipation). For those that are kept in, count the number of droppings, and if this reduces, feed a bran mash as a laxative. A one-off mash is a useful transition from a horse's normal diet to convalescence rations.

Watch for other problems

❑ A horse that is being box-rested for severe lameness is at risk of further injury such as tendon strain or laminitis as a result of the increased strain on the other legs.

❑ All the feet should be checked daily for warning signs: these might include increased warmth and digital pulse, or bruising on the sole. A deep bed that encourages the horse

to lie down will help to reduce this risk; sometimes a vet will recommend fitting frog supports on high-risk patients. The opposite leg should be support-bandaged. These bandages should include a lot of padding, and should be reset daily to check for evidence of bandage rubs, and to remove any straw or shavings that may have slipped inside the bandage.

❑ What can and cannot be fed depends on the veterinary advice given, and what is wrong with a horse. Some horses will need supplementation to encourage healing. Paradoxically the horse that cannot go out at all, is often easier to manage than one that is given a taste of freedom by being taken out for several short walks in-hand daily.

Feeding Bran

Many horseowners think bran is unsuitable, but it has some merits, especially for box rest:

Advantages

1 Proper old-fashioned broad bran holds water and can help re-hydrate a sick horse.

2 It can be an effective laxative.

3 As it passes through the gut fairly rapidly it acts as a natural detox for some sick horses, such as laminitics and some colic cases.

4 It contains some useful minerals such as selenium, magnesium and zinc.

5 It is a good way to disguise medicines that must be fed to a sick horse.

Disadvantages

1 It is low in calcium and high in phosphorus, which is the opposite to what horses need; however a one-off feed will do no harm.

2 The fibre in bran includes a relatively high proportion of indigestible lignin.

3 Broad bran, which consists of the traditional large flakes that are more nutritious, can be relatively expensive.

Emergency Situations

Collapse

If a horse is lying down and is unable to stand – if they are recumbent – there is something wrong. A normal horse lying down having a rest can happily stand up again unless he is cast – in other words, he is quite capable of getting to his feet except that some kind of external influence is preventing him from doing so; for instance when he rolls in his box and ends up wedged against the wall or under his manger (see page 114).

Another alarming emergency is when a horse suddenly keels over and falls down; some horses may stumble and fall, whilst others may faint. This is obviously a danger to both horse and rider, and a vet should be consulted. If the horse does not rapidly regain his feet, it is a veterinary emergency, and the longer a horse is down, the more damage

A horse with botulism that is unable to stand. First aid should include putting a towel under the head to protect the underlying eye

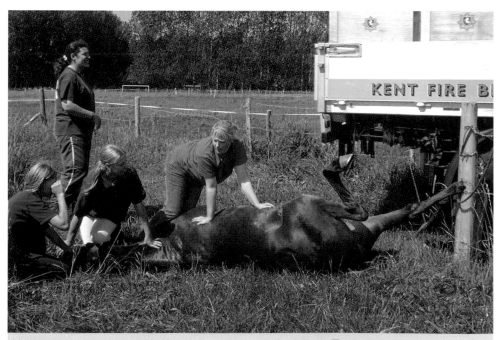

Horse anaesthetized to enable his safe removal by the fire brigade. The horse had managed to get his leg stuck between the wire and fencepost and adjacent gatepost

or deterioration that may occur. You might consider the following questions as a sort of checklist:

Is the horse breathing?

There is the awful possibility that the horse may be dead, which sounds stupidly obvious, but if you suddenly found a horse down in the field, it might be different. If you are not sure, check to see if there is any response when you touch the eye. If the eye is responsive, then check ABC – airway, breathing and circulation – and if necessary, summon help.

Is there any obvious injury, particularly to one of the limbs, that is preventing him from standing?

It can be difficult to spot a fractured limb tucked underneath the horse, particularly a shoulder.

Is there any sign of disease such as colic or laminitis, which may make the horse reluctant to stand? In these cases, with help and some persuasion, they will often get up.

If the horse is a mare, might she be foaling?

If the horse is dull and non-responsive, this might suggest some kind of brain damage. In some countries this could mean diseases such as rabies or West Nile fever; in the UK it is more likely that they have hit their head, although equine herpes infection is a possibility, or more rarely other illnesses such as botulism (illustrated).

Is there a physical obstruction that is preventing the horse from rising? You may need the vet, or the animal rescue department of the fire brigade to help. An important thing to tell them is whether the horse was normal before he went down. For instance, if he was off his feed and had a high temperature, he may have an infection. If he was galloping across the field and then fell, it is more likely an accident. It all sounds obvious when written down, but if it actually happens it can all be too stressful for you to think clearly.

Case Study: Mare is Found Recumbent

The vet receives an emergency phone call from a lady to say that she has found her beloved 25-year-old mare collapsed in the field. She can't get her up, and thinks she is dying! The vet meets a distraught owner at the edge of the field, and they drive across until the recumbent mare can be seen in the headlights through the rain. She was lying quite still on her side on a steep slope with her limbs uphill. She was soaking wet, with her rug tangled around her legs. The vet carefully checked the mare, ensured that she had normal reflexes, no temperature and no obvious signs of pain anywhere.

With difficulty the wet rug was unclipped and, by virtue of the slippery ground, pulled out from underneath the mare's body. A towel was placed under her head as support and to protect her underlying eye, and then, with two strong people pulling on the mane and someone agile pushing on the hindquarters, she was spun round the slope; everyone was careful throughout to stand behind her back to avoid being kicked. As she was moved round the slope, the mare was able to extend her forelegs in front of her, on to less slippery ground. At the same time she swung her head and neck up to balance herself and, pushing with her hind legs and with the vet supporting the tail, she struggled to her feet.

Sometimes ropes are used to roll horses over or move them round, but the utmost care must be used to keep clear of hooves, both as the horse tries to stand and when removing the ropes when they are on their feet. In this case, a check-up of the mare afterwards revealed no medical problems; she was just very fat, somewhat arthritic, and had simply got stuck: she just could not organize herself to get to her feet. She was moved to other grazing with no steep slopes and less grass, so she lost weight, and has had no further problems.

Shock

Shock is the body's response to trauma, blood loss, dehydration, pain and infection. It is a serious condition that can cause an ill horse to deteriorate rapidly. It is also a medical condition, and not a reasoned reaction: animals, including horses, do not have the capacity to rationalize circumstances they find alarming, so they will be frightened by things that we can explain and therefore do not fear. Shock is a potentially serious illness in a horse.

Signs of shock are:
- ❑ shaking and shivering;
- ❑ rapid breathing;
- ❑ a weak pulse;
- ❑ pale or blue mucous membranes;
- ❑ cold extremities: in the horse, feeling the ears is always a good guide.

These signs of shock result from the body shutting down the blood circulation. But unfortunately

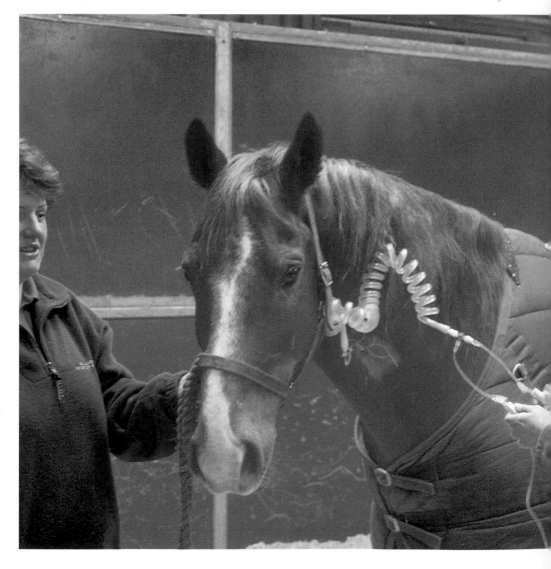

the body's natural responses can be counterproductive, and with shock, the damage becomes self-perpetuating and disastrous. Shock is frequently the killer in relation to colic, as a result of pain, stress and bacterial leakage from a twisted gut.

A horse in shock is certainly an emergency, and you would be perfectly justified in contacting your vet immediately.

Horse being treated with intravenous fluids after colic surgery to protect against shock

What to do whilst waiting for the vet:

❑ Reassuring and calming a shocked horse can help them enormously. Provided they are not likely to require an anaesthetic, food can be significantly comforting; so a full haynet can be a very effective painkiller.

❑ If the horse seems cold, give them extra rugs and warm up their extremities by putting on stable bandages all round. In a foal, a human jumper or fleece can be used in an emergency, with the sleeves pulled up over the front legs! Bring the horse into a well ventilated box, though don't close the top door as it will become too stuffy.

❑ Make sure there is water available for the horse to drink, as shock is frequently associated with dehydration.

❑ Try and establish the primary cause of the shock – for instance, it may be a wound – and treat that. If you can stop any bleeding and control the pain, the horse will quickly improve.

What your vet will do:

❑ Treatment for shock very much depends on dealing with the underlying cause. Many horses with severe colic will become shocked, so it is important to treat the underlying colic first. Serious infections can cause shock, so in this instance antibiotic and other medication should be used. If the horse is bleeding, the cause has to be found, and then the flow of blood stopped.

❑ Supportive treatment for severe shock includes the administration of fluids. If the horse cannot drink, this can mean giving large volumes of sterile fluids (40 to 80 litres per day) via an intravenous drip to combat shock and dehydration. This usually means intensive treatment in an equine hospital situation.

Wounds

Wounds are most commonly the result of accidents caused by the horse's instinct to move rapidly away from danger; they are also often caused if he gets tangled in a fence, or is kicked by another horse. Skin wounds can vary from a simple cut or puncture to a major laceration – but whatever its size, remember that any wound heals from side to side, not end to end; so even if you are faced with a nasty big hole, it can heal surprisingly well.

There are three basic steps regarding first aid with any wound:

1 Clot

2 Clean

3 Cover

First Aid for Wounds

1 Clot

Blood clotting is essential in order for bleeding to stop, and for any wound to be able to repair. A small amount of bleeding may be beneficial as it will flush dirt and debris from a wound, but severe bleeding needs to be controlled. However, remember that a little bit of blood looks worse than it is – think of the mess when even a cup of coffee is spilt on the floor! And a thoroughbred-size horse has to lose 10 to 15 litres of blood before there is a serious risk of problems.

❑ Making a pressure pad

A severed artery will spurt bright red blood, which can look alarming. Equally concerning is the persistent dark red ooze produced by a cut vein. In such cases, try to stop the bleeding by firmly applying pressure to the wound. Make a pressure pad from a thick cloth pad, or use gamgee from your first aid kit, with a non-stick dressing underneath. In an emergency use anything to hand, such as a T-shirt, a big handkerchief or a towel. Press the pad against the wound, and hold it there as tightly as possible. It is often simplest to tape it in place to keep it secure.

❑ Applying a pressure pad

Most such wounds are on the lower limb, and direct pressure over the area will control bleeding. If the blood soaks through, simply put more padding over the top and apply more pressure. You must keep a pressure pad in place for at least five minutes: do not be tempted to remove it and peep underneath, as that can restart the bleeding. This is much better than trying to use a tourniquet.

❑ Be reassuring

Talk to the horse or pony reassuringly as you keep pressure on the wound, encouraging them to stand still. If a horse is excited, the heart pumps faster, increasing the rate of bleeding. But keep them calm and still, and blood will clot more readily.

❑ Maintaining a pressure bandage

Once you have put on a firm, comfortable pressure bandage and it is controlling the bleeding, it is safe to leave it in place for up to two hours. Where a horse has incurred more than one injury, identify the main wound and get that under control; then check the horse elsewhere for the other injuries, that have been overlooked initially.

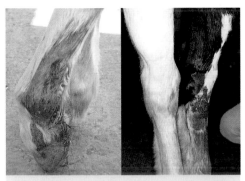

Left: Dirty wound that needs to be cleaned
Right: Wound near joint on hock

2 Clean

Cleaning any wound is important, but do not probe deeply as that can encourage infection or restart bleeding. The initial cleaning of a wound will influence the eventual healing, so it is important to remove all dirt and debris.

❑ Gentle hosing will help, as will washing with a correctly diluted antiseptic solution such as chlorhexidine (Hibiscrub®).

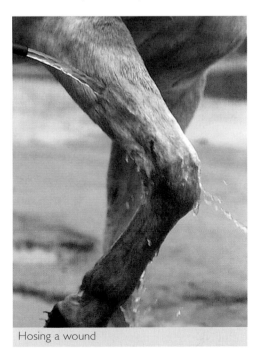

Hosing a wound

❑ In an emergency, use water. If you are worried about cleanliness, use approximately 500ml boiled water in a clean container, with a teaspoon of salt added.

❑ Small bags of sterile saline can be kept in the first aid kit, to wash out wounds.

❑ Moist wipes as manufactured for babies can be useful.

❑ How to proceed

How you decide to proceed will depend on the severity of the injury.

❑ If a wound looks awful, you should contact a vet immediately.

❑ If the damage seems minor, it will help to clean up the area and find out what exactly is going on, so that you can then give the vet more accurate information.

❑ Make sure your own hands are clean if you are touching the wound.

❑ Once you have cleaned and washed away the blood, you will often find that the injury is smaller than initially suspected.

❑ Filling a wound with a proper wound hydrogel such as IntraSite®, Dermagel® or Vetalintex® will help provide the right moist, clean environment to encourage healing.

❑ Then, if possible, trim away the hair from the edge of the wound. This allows the extent of the damage to be seen and prevents hair contaminating the wound.

❑ At this stage the two key things to assess are the anatomical position of the wound and the overall condition of the horse.

❑ The position of the wound

Be vigilant if the wound is located near a vital structure such as a joint or the digital tendon sheath at the back of the pastern (see p34). Even seemingly superficial wounds can penetrate vital structures, and can cripple a horse if they are not treated aggressively right from the start.

❑ The bones of the equine limb are relatively poorly protected by muscle, so are at risk.

- If you can see white tissue exposed within the wound, it may be tendon, ligament or bone, and you should contact a vet.
- Is the face involved? Most eyelid wounds should be surgically repaired, and other head wounds will often heal better if sutured. Obviously with any major head trauma a vet should be contacted to check for underlying damage to the nervous system.

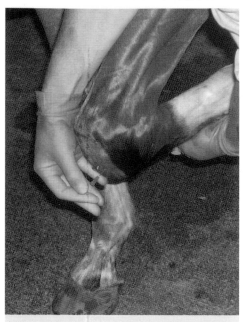

Vet checking knee joint for infection by taking a sterile sample of joint fluid

Danger site: fetlock wound

The overall condition of the horse

If the horse is lamer than you would expect for the size of the injury, or if he is more distressed than anticipated for the size of the wound, then something serious may be involved. This could be damage to a bone or joint, in which case again it requires urgent veterinary attention.

3 Cover

There is a tendency to overreact and apply ointments or powders to the wound, which can interfere with healing. If it is not safe in an eye, it should not go in a wound. Most wounds occur on the lower limb, so are best bandaged, first to protect them from muck, mud and bedding, and also to provide the warm, moist environment that encourages rapid wound healing. Use a sterile non-adherent wound dressing such as Melonin® to hold some wound gel in place, then bandage routinely (see page 20). Wounds on the upper body frequently cannot be bandaged, but should be kept as clean as possible.

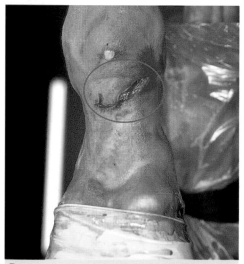

Danger site: digital sheath wound; in this case it is clipped, cleaned, and the foot covered at the start of surgery

Types of Wounds

Wounds that cause concern include lacerations, puncture wounds, and those involving the entry of a foreign body.

❏ Laceration

This is a traumatic tearing of the skin in an uncontrolled direction, and is a common equine injury. The blood vessels tend to be stretched, so bleeding is rarely a problem, although the tissues are bruised and sore. Adequate treatment is impossible until all affected structures are identified. This means that the vet 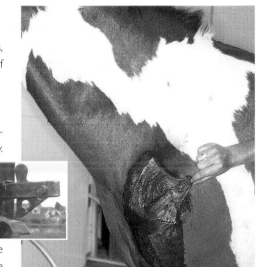 often spends a long time cleaning and preparing the wound prior to deciding whether it can be repaired immediately, or should be referred to a surgical facility. Lacerations requiring special treatment include those involving:

- ❏ tendons and tendon sheaths
- ❏ extensive skin wounds
- ❏ bone damage
- ❏ major blood vessels
- ❏ coronary band and hoof wall
- ❏ joints

Lacerations involving less critical structures are cleaned, and damaged tissue removed; they may then be stitched, or left bandaged for several days. Some will be stitched at a later stage.

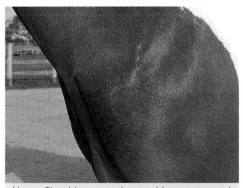

Above: Shoulder wound caused by a gate catch (see inset photo). Below: The healed wound

When to Contact a Vet

Call your vet in the following circumstances:

- ❏ When any wound is bleeding profusely.
- ❏ When a horse is very lame, even if the wound itself is small.
- ❏ When a wound is more than 6cm (2in) long and has gone right through the skin.
- ❏ If you suspect there may be a foreign body in the wound.
- ❏ If you suspect a vital structure such as a joint is involved.
- ❏ If a horse has not had an anti-tetanus vaccination.

❏ Puncture wounds

Many puncture wounds are so tiny that they are hard to see; sometimes it can be difficult to identify the injury in the first place! Frequently the first indication of a puncture wound is when swelling appears at the site. Infection can spread extensively from the original wound, and this is particularly true on a leg, where the whole limb can swell up following a simple puncture wound. Clues to look for when checking for puncture wounds are a trickle of blood on the coat, or a sensitive scab when feeling the area, associated with localized swelling. Sometimes the vet will clip hair away from the area of suspicion to see exactly what is going on.

Key points for puncture wounds: First find the injury! Be aware that small wounds can have the most serious consequences. The damage caused depends on how deep the wound is, how dirty it is, and whether it has involved any vital structures. Many more trivial superficial wounds will discharge clear or yellow serum, which can appear similar to joint fluid; but if in doubt, get it checked.

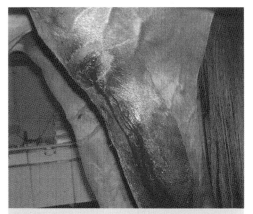

Puncture wound on the stifle of an event horse

Emergency treatment: Clip away the coat and clean around any puncture wound. Avoid spraying water, using hydrogen peroxide, or anything else that could go directly into the wound, as this may force dirt deeper. Again, hydrogels are useful to apply, and a clean bandage helps protect the wound. Traditionally poultices have been applied to puncture wounds with the aim of drawing out dirt and debris; however, a soggy poultice can encourage infection and be counterproductive. Personally I prefer to apply a clean bandage and use a hydrogel on the wound. Ice packs and cold hosing are also beneficial. This type of wound provides the ideal anaerobic (lacking in oxygen) environment for tetanus bacteria to flourish. As puncture wounds are often undetected, all horses and ponies should be routinely vaccinated against tetanus. If not properly protected, vaccination must be obtained. A properly vaccinated horse does not need a booster for every fresh wound.

Consider what caused the puncture: There is always the risk that a foreign body is still stuck inside. Be careful about introducing further infection by probing into any wound. If in doubt, ask the vet, particularly if a wound does not heal, which would suggest there is something festering inside it.

Is it really a puncture? Two puncture points close together could be a snake bite, and a hole with pus draining out may be an internal abscess that has burst. Do not underestimate a puncture wound: its small size often disguises an underlying injury of much greater potential severity, and such a wound can be fatal if it affects a vital organ such as the brain, chest, abdomen or the inside of the foot.

❏ Foreign bodies

These are a first aid dilemma. If there is a foreign body wedged in a wound, in most circumstances it is best left there until you have veterinary help, unless it is very loose. Most foreign bodies when found are truly wedged in place, otherwise they would have fallen out already! Many can be extremely difficult and potentially painful to remove, and it is much better for a vet to do this, with the help of appropriate painkillers and sedatives, and then check the injury properly. A foreign body may break off within a wound, so the site of the accident and any potential foreign bodies – for example, a splinter from broken fencing – should be noted. Wood is a high risk material, as it may splinter deep within a wound and only be detected months later, when the injury fails to heal.

Foreign bodies in the foot: Where the foot is concerned the opposite applies, in that if the horse has stood on a nail it is usually best to remove it,

---

Promoting Healing

With any wound, adequate tetanus protection and appropriate antibiotics are required. Painkillers will also help the horse. An animal that is comfortable will heal better.

before his weight pushes it in any further. The critical issue is, which part of the foot is affected (see Lameness, page 40).

Stake wounds: This type of wound has the potential to penetrate a body cavity, with the risk of a foreign body being stuck inside. Always think about what is going on inside the horse's body, rather than worrying about just the skin injury itself. Horses sometimes stake themselves on fence posts around the chest or thigh area, but as long as the chest or abdomen is not penetrated, many such wounds heal very well. Even so, you should still contact a vet urgently.

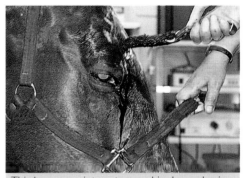

This horse ran into a tree and is shown having the large stick removed. Fortunately it missed the brain by millimetres and the horse made a full recovery

Are Stitches Necessary?

Many wounds will heal very well without stitches (sutures), and these are often not as necessary as people think. This is particularly true on equine limbs, where the blood supply is frequently poor. If it is to be stitched, a wound should meet the following criteria: It should…

❑ **Be accessible**

If, for example, it is inside the back leg and the horse kicks, it will not be possible to do a decent job without heavy sedation or even general anaesthesia.

❑ **Be clean and fresh**

If you do not find the injury until the day after and the skin edges are dried up, it is unlikely it will be improved by suturing.

❑ **Have the blood supply intact**

A vet will be the one to decide this, but many jagged lacerations, especially upward-pointing flaps on the limb, do not mend well.

❑ **Have enough skin to hold together without tension**

Where there is excessive motion – for instance, at the front of the knee, where the wound will move every time the leg bends – the chances of stitches staying in place are poor. Sometimes vets will apply a very heavy bandage, or will cast the leg in order to minimize bending.

❑ **Be without infection**

An infected wound is not going to heal easily. Wounds with severe bruising from impact injuries are more likely to become seriously infected than are, say, lacerations caused by sharp objects; because of this tendency they are often best not stitched.

The best wound to stitch is the fresh, clean cut that has just happened. Most horse wounds are dirty and not ideal to suture; however, the vet looking at the horse must decide. Never pressure a vet into suturing a wound in an emergency: it is far better to ensure the wound is clean and healthy by leaving it open to drain. It may be possible to repair some wounds days after the initial injury, when swelling and contamination have been reduced. Such delayed repair is often underused, as everyone wants an immediate solution. Remember that wounds shrink, and this will help healing, especially in ponies. Wounds below the hock and the knee in big horses can be slow to heal, and will need good nursing. They will often need bandaging as protection to help healing.

Poisoning

A poison is any substance that causes injury or death if ingested, inhaled, absorbed, or injected in sufficient quantity. Examples of the more common poisons include:

- **bacterial:** botulism, tetanus
- **chemical:** lead-, smoke-, feed-associated poisoning, such as antibiotic and other substances in feed for farm stock, but fed to horses
- **plants:** bracken, ragwort (below left), foxgloves, yew (below right), horsetail or marestail, water hemlock

Symptoms of Poisoning

Suspicion of poisoning is high when a horse becomes ill for no obvious reason, though in fact a more straightforward cause usually exists. A diagnosis of poisoning should only be made if a horse was clearly seen to have been in contact with the substance in question.

Poisoning can cause a variety of clinical signs, including collapse, colic, constriction or dilation of the pupils of the eyes, convulsions, depression, diarrhoea, difficulty swallowing and/or breathing, excitement, loss of appetite, muscle tremors, muscle weakness, staggering, sweating, sudden death.

The amount of material the horse has been exposed to, and over what possible time period, is important. Samples of suspect feedstuffs or other materials should be collected promptly so that tests can be run, although there is no one screen that can be used to test for every possibility. Analysis can be costly and unproductive. A vet should be contacted as soon as poisoning is suspected. Many poisons act quickly: for instance, the horse is extremely susceptible to yew toxicity, and one mouthful can be fatal within as little as five minutes.

Basic First Aid Management

The following steps should be taken in the event of a suspected or confirmed case of poisoning:

- Prevent any further exposure, and in the case of chemicals, this should include people as well.
- Establish whether other animals are affected or at risk. It is more likely to be poisoning if several horses are sick and there is no sign of an infection.
- Delay further absorption and encourage elimination of the poison. A vet may administer substances such as activated charcoal or Epsom salts by stomach tube.

- Give specific treatment. Effective antidotes are rare in horses.
- Give supportive treatment, such as plenty to drink, and keep the horse warm and comfortable.
- In cases of skin exposure, the coat should be washed with a mild detergent and plenty of water.

The following web sites contain excellent pictures to identify plants that may be poisonous:

http://www.bhs.org.uk/welfare_leaflets/poisonous-plants.htm
http://www.caf.wvu.edu/~forage/library/poisonous/content.htm
http://www.hsc.wvu.edu/charleston/wvpc/toxic_plants.html

Burns and Scalds

Both burn and scald injuries are thankfully rare in horses; when they do happen they are most often the result of a barn or stable fire. However, they can also be due to:

- Water scalds
- Friction burns, for example from ropes or rugs
- Chemical or caustic burns
- Freeze burns, usually from over-enthusiastic ice therapy
- Sunburn

The back of the head and ears, and the upper side of the neck and body are most frequently involved in a barn fire.

Classification of Burns

The seriousness of a burn depends on the depth and size of the area affected. The hair may be singed or absent, and the burn damage to the skin is classified in three degrees:

- **Superficial or first degree:** The damaged skin will be red, moist and smooth, and very tender. If you touch it, the skin goes white.
- **Partial thickness or second degree:** As above, but with blisters.
- **Full thickness or third degree:** The skin varies in colour from white, to red, to black, and it looks dry and leathery. It is not sore because the nerve endings are burnt, and when you press it, it does not go white.

Generally, the higher the degree of burn and broader the skin damage, the more likelihood of shock, dehydration and infection. Heat and smoke also affect the rest of the body, particularly the eyes and lungs; smoke inhalation can be more serious than burns, causing severe breathing difficulties. If a horse is involved in a fire, call a vet immediately after contacting the emergency services.

Basic First Aid Management for Burns

- Remove the source of the burn: for instance, if a horse is scalded with hot water, pour on cold; if it is sunburn, go into a stable.
- Cool the affected area with ice or cold water to draw the heat out of the tissues and so arrest and reduce damage.
- Never apply grease or ointments to burns.
- Full-thickness burns should be covered immediately with a protective, fluid-proof dressing. In an emergency, clear plastic kitchen wrap can be useful. Ideally a layer of wound gel (hydrogel) should be applied directly to the wound.
- With chemical burns, management will entail removal of the substance by gentle but copious appropriate washing, then providing suitable topical medication. It may help to clip the entire area of damage to prevent the coat matting and harbouring infection.
- With burns, any blisters should not be burst, but you should wait for a vet, who will apply soothing antibacterial creams and dress the wounds. This is crucial if horses are involved in a field fire and their limbs are burnt. In stable fires where the horse's back is burnt, sometimes it may help if a cotton sheet soaked in mild antiseptic is draped over their topline. The vet will prescribe painkillers and sometimes antibiotics, and if necessary will also treat the horse for shock.

Assessing Lameness

It is useful in an emergency to determine whether a horse can bear any weight on the injured limb. If the leg is broken the horse will simply not be able to stand on it at all. With foot pain – and this is the most common kind of lameness – and especially with a foot abscess, a horse may try to stand on the foot but will then hurriedly lift it up, as any weight on the tender spot will be painful.

To check how lame a horse is, it is useful to see it walk and trot with its head held loosely, so any head nod can be detected

When to Contact a Vet

The severity of the lameness, and the level of pain, should help you decide when you should call your vet.

❑ If the horse is standing on only three legs and cannot walk at all, call the vet immediately.

❑ If he has suddenly become noticeably lame, for instance overnight or with a wound, call the vet the same day.

❑ If he can walk on the lame leg, but prefers to rest it, call a vet within 24 hours; the situation would appear to be less critical, nevertheless the horse should be seen with minimal delay.

❑ A gradually worsening lameness is perhaps when it is hardest to decide when to call a vet, as it may slowly become a serious problem. If it does not respond to a few days' rest, and cannot be resolved by the farrier checking the foot, then it is time to call a vet.

❑ Any suspicion of lameness means that a horse should not be worked.

Foot Pain

Pain in the foot is the commonest cause of lameness – even pain that appears to be in the shoulder usually originates in the foot! Quite often the affliction is 'pus in the foot', properly called a sub-solar abscess.

A bruised foot will present as a similar sort of foot lameness. A corn, which is always painful, is a bruise on the heel at the so-called seat of corn. The vet or farrier will need to examine the foot carefully to work out what is happening, then drain pus or pare out a bruise.

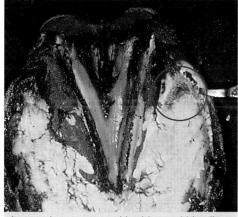

A corn shows up as red bruising and bleeding

Pus in the Foot

This type of infection in the hoof is particularly prevalent in wet weather following a dry spell. Dry weather causes the hoof wall to dry out, and tiny cracks then appear; when the weather changes, moisture, dirt and bacteria track up through these cracks, and infection then rapidly develops, the end result being an extremely painful build-up of pus within the confines of the hoof.

How to recognize it

Initially the lameness may be only slight, but gradually it becomes so bad that the poor horse can barely walk; sometimes he will only put the toe to the ground in an effort to avoid putting any more pressure on the foot as this causes great pain. Other signs include:

❑ heat in the affected hoof – it may feel warmer than the other feet;

❑ a prominent pulse to the foot;

❑ pain: there is sometimes quite severe distress and discomfort;

❑ swelling up the leg, which can be confused with a tendon injury.

If the abscess is not drained from the bottom of the foot, the pus will work its way up the hoof wall and eventually burst out at the coronary band.

What to do

❑ If pus in the foot is suspected, arrange for the farrier or vet to see the horse as soon as possible. The shoe may need to be removed to find the pus, but once the abscess is located and the pus drained, the horse should improve.

❑ Poulticing the hard horn to soften it can encourage the abscess to burst. Avoid poulticing around the coronary band (unless that is where the pus has broken out), as a hot poultice will burn the skin; also it is best to encourage the infection to drain downwards, rather than to burst open at the coronary band – the pus doesn't always drain fully if it goes upwards, and the abscess will tend to recur.

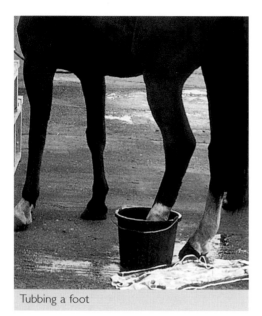

Tubbing a foot

- ❑ The traditional method of cleaning the foot was to stand the horse with his hoof in a tub of warm water with either table salt or Epsom salts added. The vet or farrier will advise as to how best to clean the actual area of the abscess; it may require flushing with hydrogen peroxide or an antiseptic preparation.
- ❑ Keep the abscess site covered with a dressing until it has healed sufficiently to prevent further dirt entering the foot. Never use a wet poultice for more than three days, as the hoof will go soft.
- ❑ Keep the horse stabled, particularly when the foot is bandaged; a disposable nappy will make a very effective and simple bandage in an emergency.
- ❑ Applying a mixture of 4 parts sugar and 1 part pevidine inside a foot dressing can be a cheap and effective way of reducing infection.

Foreign Bodies in the Foot

A horse that has stood on a nail is a common emergency. Most of these are minor injuries and recover rapidly, but a deep puncture wound can be crippling. If you find a nail in your horse's foot, you should note the following:

- ❑ where the nail penetrated the foot;
- ❑ the angle it went in;
- ❑ how deep it went in – how much of the length of the nail is within the foot.

If the nail is removed, mark the point of entry – and always take care when removing any foreign body to ensure it does not break off as it is removed. In theory it is sensible to leave foreign bodies where they have become wedged, until you have professional help to remove them; however, a nail in the foot is the one exception to this rule, since at every step

the horse may push the nail in further. If a nail goes more than 2cm into the foot, do not delay before contacting your vet.

The deeper the nail goes, the more dangerous it is, particularly if it happens to pierce the middle third of the foot, which is the critical zone where several vital structures are located: the navicular bone and associated structures, the deep digital flexor tendon and its sheath, and the coffin joint.

A nail run into the toe of a horse's foot may infect or break the pedal bone. Heel wounds result in infection in that area, but are rarely life-threatening. If a dirty foreign body such as a nail reaches any vital structures, aggressive treatment is required and poulticing is unlikely to be enough. Punctures to the foot can be deceptive, as they look so much better when the nail is removed; consequently treatment may be delayed until it is too late. In these cases pain is not always a clear indicator that something serious is wrong, or that the situation may deteriorate.

What to do:

❑ Treat superficial punctures by scrubbing the site with antiseptic, and ask a vet about flushing the wound with dilute hydrogen peroxide.

❑ Always apply a clean dressing, poultice or use a

sugardine (4 parts sugar: 1 part pevidine) mixture inside the dressing.

❑ A deep puncture in the middle third of the foot needs to be seen by a vet urgently.

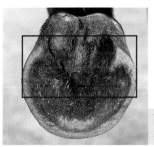

The 'danger zone'

Lameness after Shoeing

Sometimes a horseshoe nail will touch the sensitive tissues of the foot, causing temporary lameness: this is known as 'nail bind' or a 'pricked foot'. It is more likely to happen if the horse is badly behaved and will not stand still for the

farrier, or if it has a particularly poor hoof structure with a thin outer hoof wall.

What to do

❑ Ask the farrier to remove the shoe if necessary; certainly the offending nail must be removed.

❑ Use a hoof supplement to improve horn quality.

Interference Injuries

The damage that is caused when one leg hits another is known as an 'interference injury'. The most common is an overreach, where the hind leg strikes into the back of the front pastern or heels; such an injury is common in deep going as this inhibits easy limb clearance, or in lively animals that trip up on their own feet! Overreach boots can help prevent such injuries. Overreach injuries can result in a sudden severe lameness; at best they are associated with bruising to the heels, and at worse they cause a large open wound. Any such wound is going to be dirty, and the horse may be surprisingly sore.

The best first aid is to apply wound gel to the area of damage, and then apply a clean bandage. In serious cases, consult the vet.

Overreach boots

Laminitis

Laminitis is an agonizing condition that affects the feet, and unfortunately it is a common emergency. However, the chances of recovery are maximized if treatment is started early. Basically laminitis can occur in two forms: acute and chronic.

Acute laminitis needs prompt and effective treatment. It is the early stage of the condition when the horse or pony is uncomfortable and showing lameness, but when major changes have not yet happened within the foot.

Chronic laminitis is when the pedal bone has rotated or sunk. These cases are not necessarily such an immediate emergency, but a vet should be contacted if the horse or pony is in pain. They should never be forced to walk.

Symptoms of Laminitis

In severe cases of laminitis the feet are so painful that the horse or pony is reluctant to move, or may not even want to stand. This is obviously urgent and a vet needs to be called immediately. These are the signs you should look out for:

❑ Hooves that feel hot, and feet that are painful when pressure is applied to the sole.

❑ A tendency to stand with the front legs stretched forwards, but the body leaning backwards in an attempt to shift the weight off the front feet.

❑ In milder cases the horse will appear uncertain as to which foot to stand on, so is constantly shifting the weight around because whichever foot he stands on hurts.

❑ Severe cases spend a lot of time lying down.

❑ The horse/pony may tremble, and look stressed and anxious.

❑ The intense pain associated with severe laminitis means that the pulse and respiratory rates rise. Frequently a prominent pulse is obvious where the digital artery – that takes the blood to the foot – runs over the fetlock. In a severe case this pulse will be pounding in all four feet.

Mild, chronic laminitis is much less obvious, and can be confused with other sorts of lameness. The

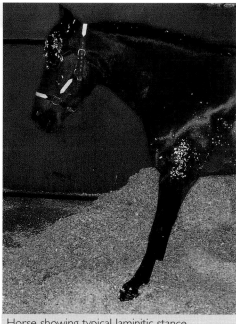

Horse showing typical laminitic stance

following characteristics may be indicative of this sort of laminitis:

❑ The pony that is 'feeling his feet', and may be intermittently lame, especially on rough ground.

❑ They are often footsore or lame after trimming.

❑ They may have odd-shaped feet with rings in the hoof wall; they may be wider at the heel than

Laminitis can occur as a result of another condition such as Cushing's disease, as with this pony

at the toe, which produces a foot with long toes. Very often the soles have dropped, the white line is wider than normal, and the feet are flat.

❑ Pus in the foot is a common complication because of the weak horn growth in the diseased hoof.

❑ There is visible red bruising within the hoof, particularly when the farrier trims the feet.

❑ This condition is most common in fat ponies, but any horse that is overweight carries an increased risk of becoming laminitic. Brood mares can be prone to laminitis.

First Aid Management

❑ Contact the vet: severe cases will need painkillers and other treatment urgently. Mild chronic cases will need a planned campaign of action involving both the vet and the farrier.

❑ If laminitis is suspected, never force the horse or pony to walk, which was the old-fashioned treatment. Allow him to lie down and rest his feet.

❑ Standing in cold water, or cold hosing will provide some short-term relief to the sore feet.

❑ Stable on deep, non-edible bedding such as shavings, paper or sand that will mould to the feet and help to support them.

❑ It is possible to tape special frog supports on to the feet to help. There are now several types of these tape-on frog supports available, ranging from purpose-designed pads or rubber wedges, to home-made bandage supports. Properly designed frog supports can be obtained (www.laminitisclinic.org) for emergency use, but it may be simpler to provide a deep soft bed and contact your vet for advice.

❑ Prevention is far better than first aid for laminitis cases. In the overweight or overfed animal, a carefully controlled diet, increased exercise and good, regular farriery are the obvious, but not easy answers. If the laminitis developed as a result of another condition, such as Cushing's disease or after foaling, that also needs proper management.

Tendon and Ligament Injuries

An injured tendon is potentially as serious as a broken bone. The signs of damage may be subtle and include:

- ❑ lameness;
- ❑ heat;
- ❑ swelling of the leg;
- ❑ thickening of the tendon;
- ❑ pain on finger pressure;
- ❑ dropping of the fetlock.

Some horses can have a serious injury with very few obvious signs, whereas others will be very sore with an enormous leg. In the case of the first scenario, even if the horse is not lame, significant tendon damage may have occurred. If there is an open wound or the horse is in pain, the vet should also be contacted immediately; otherwise it should be examined by a vet within a few days and before he is exercised or turned out, which could cause further damage.

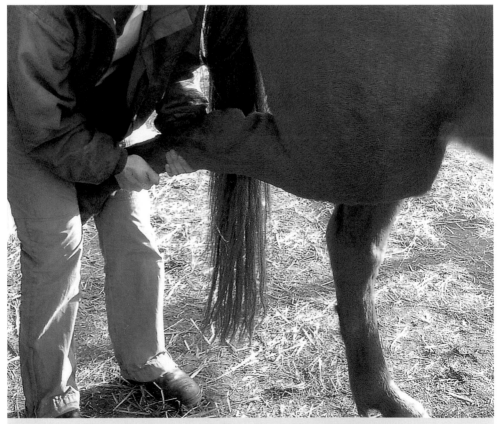

Leg at an unusual angle as a result of a ruptured ligament in the back leg. It is not recommended to stand behind a horse in this way, but in this instance the horse could not use the leg fully

First Aid Management for Suspected Tendon Damage

Cold therapy

As soon as you can, apply cold treatment and support bandaging to reduce inflammation, as this will minimize damage to the tendon fibres. Immediately following injury, treatment should be initiated with 20 minutes application of cold therapy. This is to minimize the damage to the tendon fibres and maximize the chance of a satisfactory repair. It is now thought that cold hosing (also known as hydrotherapy) is more efficient and safer at cooling the injury, than applying ice. However, if you are out somewhere with no access to a hose, holding an ice pack against the limb can be beneficial, providing you do not make the area too cold and cause a 'freeze burn'. There are proprietary chemical cooling wraps available to do this, which are a useful item to include in a travelling first aid kit for use where there is no hose. In an emergency situation, packs of frozen peas or bags of ice may be held against the limb though this should never be for longer than 30 minutes.

Support bandaging

A support bandage will help limit swelling and relieve pain. You may need veterinary advice for bandaging, but as a rule of thumb, the more padding and support, the better. It is also very important to bandage the other leg for support.

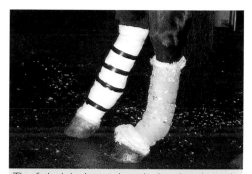

The fetlock is dropped on the bandaged purple limb due to a severe tendon injury

Anti-inflammatory medication

With any severe tendon injury the amount of inflammation will be reduced and the horse will feel better if anti-inflammatory, pain-killing medication can be given as soon as possible. Ideally it should be administered directly into the vein by the vet, so it starts to work at once. Powders given in the feed will take longer to have an effect.

Rest

Rest is beneficial for any tendon injury, often combined with controlled exercise. Do not work the horse until the severity of the injury is known: continuing to work a horse with even a mild tendon injury may be catastrophic.

Assessing the damage

❑ Look at the horse's stance: if the fetlock is closer to the ground than normal (see photo top right and opposite), or if the toe is pointing upwards, it indicates there is a major tendon rupture and the vet should be contacted immediately. Also watch for pain and swelling.

❑ Diagnostic ultrasound scanning is a useful means of estimating the severity of a tendon injury, and should be considered if there is any suspicion of damage.

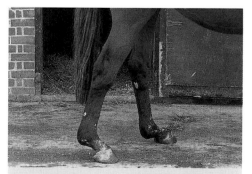

Brood mare suspensory collapse: both fetlocks are closer than normal to the ground

Fractures

Every horse owner's nightmare is their horse going suddenly and severely lame due to a fracture. Fortunately, in reality the cause is generally more likely to be a problem in the foot, such as an overreach or abscess. However, there are certain indicative factors that are characteristic of a broken bone:

❏ Sudden non-weight-bearing lameness: the horse cannot use the leg at all.
❏ A loud crack is heard prior to the onset of lameness.
❏ The limb is totally unstable and may dangle at an unusual angle.
❏ The horse is in extreme pain.

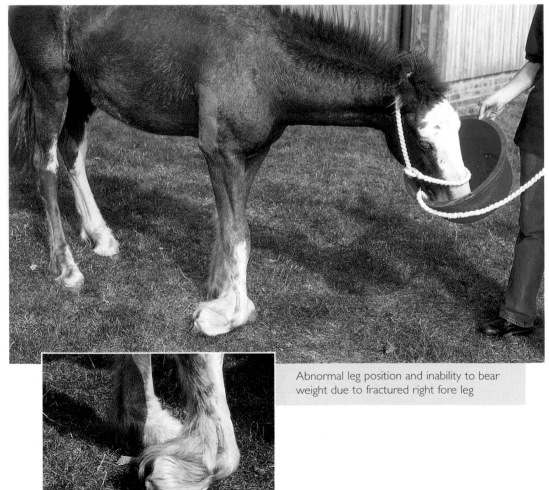

Abnormal leg position and inability to bear weight due to fractured right fore leg

What To Do

You should request an immediate emergency visit from the vet, explaining the seriousness of the situation. In the meantime you can help the horse in the following ways:

❑ Keep them as quiet and as still as possible.

❑ Cover them with a coat or rug to keep them warm, as they will be shocked.

❑ If loose in the field, catch them quietly and prevent them from moving, to minimize further damage. Never give chase if they run off.

❑ Food is often a good calming measure: try offering hay and a bucket of feed. This is not ideal for any subsequent anaesthetic, but that may be hours ahead, and the immediate requirement is to restrict movement as much as possible.

❑ Arranging transportation will save time later. A horse with a leg injury will find it easier to walk up the gentler slope of a trailer ramp than a steeper horsebox ramp. Alternatively position the lorry down a slope so the ramp is more level. Racecourses and other equine facilities have special horse ambulances for this purpose.

❑ A good supporting splint and an easy journey with a good driver will minimize further damage, and this can sometimes make a significant difference to the final outcome.

Types of Fracture

Fractures of the equine limb bones can be put into the following basic categories:

Obvious catastrophic broken bones

These are mostly fractures of a long bone, across the main supporting shaft of the limb. These bones have a vital weight-bearing role, so a fracture here is usually a disaster. Generally they are impossible to repair, particularly in anything larger than a small pony. If there is an open wound with bone sticking out through the skin, then the tissue damage and infection will be overwhelming.

Less obvious broken bones

These are usually fractures of a small bone, such as those within the hock, the knee or the foot. Treatment depends on the size of the fragment, the angle of the fracture plane, and the degree of joint involvement. Some, such as splint bone injuries, may be treatable, with the injured horse returning to full work.

Fractures that are not at all obvious

These include hairline cracks that have not displaced. Usually they heal as long as the bones do

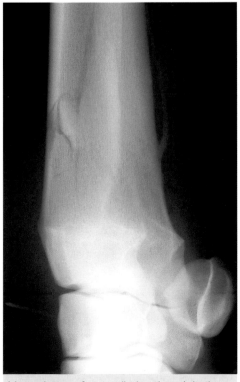

X-ray picture of a non-displaced crack in the radius

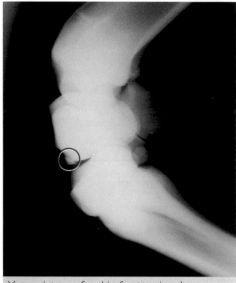

X-ray picture of a chip fracture in a knee

not suffer displacement, when they will transform into an obvious catastrophic fracture. Stress or fatigue fractures are most commonly found in young thoroughbred racehorses, and can rarely be diagnosed simply by examining the horse. A particular problem with these cases is that the horse may be only transiently lame; consequently they may be turned out or returned to work long before the damage has repaired, resulting in further and more serious injury. This is a good reason for getting a vet to check any lame horse thoroughly with X-ray pictures.

Chip fractures

These occur when a small fragment of bone becomes detached. The effect of this may only be trivial at some sites, but a bone chip in a joint can cause crippling arthritis.

Obtaining a Diagnosis

Limb injuries that would justify immediate euthanasia include:
❑ multiple fractures;
❑ complete upper hind-limb or forelimb fractures (involving the tibia, femur or humerus), except possibly in lightweight miniature ponies such as Shetlands or Caspians;
❑ complete radial (the long bone above the knee) fractures in patients weighing more than a large pony;
❑ compound comminuted fractures: bone breaks with open wounds and many fragments;
❑ severe, long-standing infection of a joint, synovial sheath or bursa;
❑ severe loss or damage to soft tissues.

With most other injuries there is usually more time to consider the treatment options available. Nasty injuries, such as a fracture of the point of the elbow, can be successfully mended even in larger horses.

Obtaining a clear diagnosis can be surprisingly difficult even in an extremely lame horse. It may be necessary to move the horse to an equine hospital facility to establish the cause, and with adequate splinting and good pain relief it is possible to make the journey comfortable. Without moving the horse it may be impossible to make a diagnosis, and consequently there would be the risk of a horse being destroyed without knowing if treatment were feasible.

Regrettably many fractures in the horse are untreatable. Some limb fractures are potentially repairable, but require a long and costly course of surgical treatment. In many cases rapid euthanasia is the kindest option. It is worth considering what you and your insurers would choose to do before being faced with such a crisis. If you are not the owner, try to contact them, so that they can discuss the situation with the vet.

Locking Stifle

This sudden severe lameness can be confused with a broken leg or pus in the foot. It is properly known as 'upward fixation of the patella', and mostly occurs in the following groups of horses:

- ❑ Young, immature animals that are not in regular work.
- ❑ Horses that have been taken out of training and confined to a stable, often as a result of illness or injury.
- ❑ Some breeds, particularly small ponies such as Shetlands.

Locking stifle, easily confused with a broken leg at first glance

Symptoms

- ❑ A sudden severe lameness, never during exercise, but during box rest or at the start of movement. It is usually seen as the horse walks out of his stable.
- ❑ The affected back leg will point backwards and appear unable to bend fully. The animal may hop forwards, dragging the toe along the ground with a slightly bent fetlock.
- ❑ It may click back to normal after a few strides, or it may persist for longer. Mostly it is intermittent,

with affected horses moving relatively normally, and then occasionally the stifle will get caught up for a few strides.

- ❑ The equine mechanism for sleeping standing up involves the patella or kneecap catching over the end of the thigh bone. Normally a horse can unlock or free their patella, but occasionally it catches: hence the name. The leg may appear stuck at an odd angle, hence the confusion with a fracture.

First Aid Management

- ❑ Check that the leg is stuck backward, rather than hanging at an odd angle. The horse or pony is unlikely to be distressed, whereas a fracture is obviously painful. Frequently the patella will free itself after a few strides, and it is often possible to make it unlock by:
  - making the horse move forwards suddenly;
  - making them back;
  - manipulating the stifle.
- ❑ Immature, unfit or poorly muscled animals will

frequently grow out of this irregularity as they become older and stronger; most are improved by increasing fitness, regular exercise and good foot care. If it keeps happening, consult the vet, as surgery is a possibility.

- ❑ Discuss special shoes with the vet and farrier. Individuals vary, but often it helps if the farrier can slightly raise the heels, shorten the toes, and lower the medial wall a fraction more than the lateral one.

Illness and Disease

Colic

Colic refers to any sort of abdominal pain, and can affect horses and ponies of all ages and types. It is a veterinary emergency that every horse owner dreads. However, understanding the possible causes of the condition, and planning ahead, can reduce the trauma. Unfortunately there is a need to be prepared, since colic is a relatively common disease. Certain factors have been recognized that increase the chance of colic occurring; these include:

❑ sudden changes in diet;
❑ a high concentrate diet;
❑ restricted access to water;
❑ poor parasite control;
❑ a change in management.

All these factors are linked to feeding and management. It has been known for years that horses are naturally designed to be grazing animals, yet we stable them, feed them a high concentrate diet, and limit their access to grazing to small paddocks frequently contaminated with droppings, where they will be more at risk of picking up parasites: no wonder they develop gut ache! Good management and sensible parasite control will reduce these risks: your vet can advise you on the modern approaches to worm control – nowadays there are more useful things you can do to protect your horse, rather than randomly squirting a different wormer paste down their throat every couple of months.

When a horse has serious colic, owners frequently wonder what they have done wrong; however, many colics are in fact unavoidable. Despite impeccable management and rigorous parasite control, some horses will still end up having surgery with no one and nothing to blame except their own inbuilt design faults and bad luck! The average-size horse has approximately 22m of small intestine, loosely anchored in the abdomen. There are another 4m of large colon, folded in several U-bends, plus a metre or so of caecum on top of that. Both large and small bowel have a high potential to twist, telescope or otherwise become entangled. Increased risk factors for a colic to require surgery include:

❑ previous colic surgery;
❑ increasing age;
❑ poor parasite control.
❑ It has also been shown that geldings have a slightly increased risk of developing a surgical colic. This may reflect the inevitable scarring and changes that can occur after even the most carefully performed castration.

Recent research has shown a background incidence of 0.1 to 0.2 episodes per horse per year, which means that if you have ten horses you should expect one to two cases of colic every year; though any more than this would be abnormally high and should be checked out.

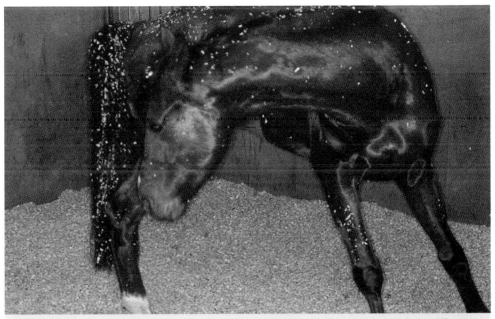

A horse with colic may frequently look at his flanks, and have bedding on the coat from rolling

Signs of Colic

It is crucial to recognize when your horse has colic, because it is a potentially dangerous emergency. There are many different causes; some are simply indigestion, which resolve with no treatment, whilst others can be life threatening, requiring rapid skilled surgery to produce a cure. Signs of colic include:

❏ restlessness: repeatedly get up and down so the horse is covered in bedding
❏ turning to look at the flank;
❏ kicking at the abdomen;
❏ sweating;
❏ rolling;
❏ pawing the ground, and digging up the bed continuously or intermittently;
❏ lying down for longer than normal;
❏ curling the top lip;
❏ repeated stretching, as if trying to urinate;
❏ dropping suddenly to the floor and/or rolling repeatedly;
❏ buckling at the knees as if trying to lie down;
❏ failure to pass any droppings in a day.

A horse with colic pain may repeatedly try to stretch, as if trying to stale

With a violent colic, the affected horse is clearly in severe pain, and something needs to be done to relieve this immediately. In such cases it is obvious that the vet should be called straightaway. It is sensible to contact your vet if even mild colic signs persist for more than half an hour.

What To Do

❑ If a colic case is violent, it is essential to ensure you are not injured.

❑ Try to calm the horse, as many will panic with the pain.

❑ Getting the horse up and walking them, particularly on hard ground, for instance concrete, where they are less likely to want to roll, may help in the short term.

❑ If they are determined to go down, make sure they have a big enough box with a deep bed, where they will not get cast. Ensure they cannot injure themselves on fittings such as mangers or buckets. Alternatively turn them out in a sand school or field, where they cannot damage themselves. Although not ideal, rolling is unlikely to make colic worse. By the time they roll, the guts may already be twisted and it is nature's way of attempting to relieve the problem. It is a myth that rolling will cause a twisted gut.

❑ It is wrong to try to walk a colicing horse for hours, as this will only exhaust them and will not cure severe pain. Walking should only be an interim measure whilst waiting for the vet. Let the horse lie down if they will do so quietly.

❑ Remove all feed from the horse's reach.

❑ Colic drenches should not be given without contacting a vet first.

❑ Have clean water, soap and towel ready for the vet when they arrive.

❑ If the colic is severe and possibly surgical, the horse may need to be transported to an equine hospital for observation and treatment, so make sure you have transport available. Decide if you would want to travel your horse for further treatment and possible surgery. Familiarize yourself with your insurance policy so you know what cover you have for colic.

What to Tell the Vet

❑ Try taking the horse's pulse; if it consistently remains over 80 beats per minute, then the horse is in serious pain.

❑ Have all information ready for the vet, particularly anything that relates to the horse's recent history, such as a change in diet or previous episodes of colic.

What Your Vet Will Do

❑ A vet will have to decide whether a colic case needs medical treatment or surgery. Most cases are medical and should respond to pain-killing medication. Somewhere between 5 and 10 per cent will be surgical, requiring emergency surgery to survive. The vet's problem is knowing which colic case fits into which category, as in the early stages the clinical signs are the same. It is impossible to diagnose the cause of colic purely on the basis of the horse's behaviour.

❑ The vet will do a detailed clinical examination, such as checking abdominal activity by listening for gut sounds. With a serious surgical colic there will be few or no normal gut sounds.

❑ The vet often performs a rectal or internal examination to help diagnose the cause of the colic. They may also take a sample of fluid from inside the abdomen; this is known as a belly tap or peritoneal tap (right). By looking at

the fluid, your vet will have another clue as to what is wrong, and if surgery is required.

❑ Sometimes a stomach tube is passed to relieve pressure in the stomach and to allow the administration of large volumes of liquid paraf-

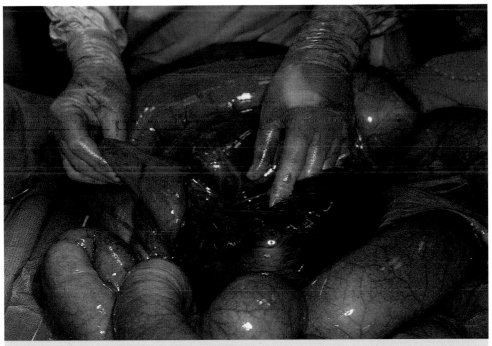

Surgery in close-up: the dark red is twisted dead small intestine, which is being separated out prior to removal

fin or other substances. Horses cannot vomit, and passing a stomach tube will allow gas and fluid to escape, so preventing a build-up of pressure and a potentially fatal rupture of the stomach.

❏ The few cases that do require surgery may temporarily appear to improve with painkillers, particularly certain medications that are so strong that they can disguise extreme pain. Even so, such horses will deteriorate and die without emergency surgical repair. It can be very hard to distinguish whether or not surgery is necessary. If there is any doubt, then it is usually safer to transport the horse to an equine hospital, so he is in the right place if he deteriorates.

❏ When an abdominal crisis occurs in a horse, there is no time to lose. If you are lucky, a lorry ride to the veterinary clinic may help cure the colic, and if the horse is better on arrival, no one will complain. Once at an equine hospital

accustomed to dealing with colics, the case can be reassessed and monitored to determine the best course of action. The vets can then perform further tests, such as abdominal ultrasound examination and laboratory tests as required.

❏ It is crucially important for the horse owner to recognize as soon as possible that the horse has a colic that requires veterinary attention.

❏ Colic is best controlled if treatment is started early on – if it requires surgical intervention, it has a much better chance of success if surgery is performed promptly. Every vet dreads the early morning call to the horse found colicing that may have been in agony all night. Regular checks on the horses under your care will allow early detection of any problems. It is particularly important to keep checking a horse after a bout of colic to see if it recurs. What was initially a bout of mild discomfort may recur more severely.

What Chance of Survival?

Apart from the serious condition of grass sickness, the majority of medical colics will respond successfully to treatment. You can assume that, at present, a horse with surgical colic will have about a 75 per cent chance of survival, provided that he gets to the hospital quickly, and that the surgery is undertaken by an experienced team. Some equine hospitals claim higher survival rates than this, but this depends on how the figures are worked out and the type of case load. Obviously the horse that has been sick for more than a day before he reaches a clinic has a much poorer chance of survival than one that is presented for surgery immediately.

Management After Surgery

Many horses that have undergone successful colic surgery return to full work. After colic surgery there can be skin sutures that will need removing after 10 to 14 days. The horse may need a special diet, and he will need restricted exercise (box rest and walking in hand) for at least 4 weeks; this is required to give the abdominal wound a chance to heal. After that time, the horse may be turned out into a small paddock for a further 4 to 8 weeks. Return to training or exercise should not take place for 2 to 3 months. Precise details about the management and timing of return to work need to be discussed with the vet because they will vary from case to case, but every colic surgery case will require a significant period of time off work.

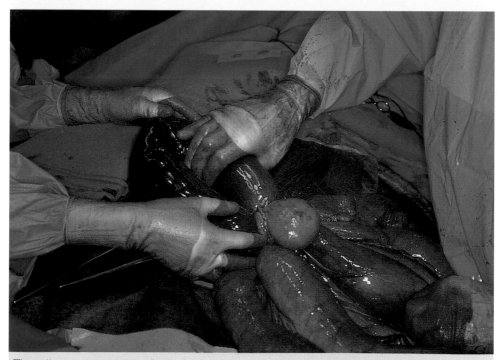

The yellow mass is a benign fatty growth on a stalk (a pedunculated lipoma) that has tangled the gut causing surgical colic. It is a relatively common condition in older horses

CASE EXAMPLES

The Need for Speed

Victoria, a large Irish sport horse mare, started colicing suddenly one Saturday. Within the space of an hour she rapidly became very uncomfortable, and the pain got worse despite the vet's treatment of large doses of painkillers. Her lack of response to this medication, and the fact that the vet could feel a distended large bowel on rectal examination, indicated that the mare needed surgery. She was fortunate that she was less than an hour from an equine hospital, so she was on the operating table within three hours of the first sign of pain. This speed saved her because she had a twist of the large colon, and would have died in as little as eight hours had she not been able to have urgent surgery.

After surgery she needed intensive aftercare, and was on a drip for two days. Once she was home she was box rested for eight weeks before being turned out on restricted grazing. It was six months before she could return to work. Thankfully she made a full recovery.

False Colic

Thomas was a much loved riding horse. One Sunday evening he was noticed kicking at his belly and looking uncomfortable; but as it was late and he seemed only mildly disturbed, his owner lunged him and then gave him painkillers by mouth, plus a swig of whisky to see if that would make him settle. But when after a couple of hours he did not improve, the vet was called. A careful examination eventually revealed that he was actually kicking at his sheath, and that he was suffering from an infestation of maggots; it was therefore a false colic, and nothing to do with abdominal pain!

Diarrhoea

Diarrhoea can occur with or without colic. If an adult horse with diarrhoea is bright, well, and eating and drinking happily, it is unlikely to be an immediate emergency. Nevertheless, you should contact a vet if it continues for more than 48 hours. A foal with diarrhoea justifies contacting the vet the same day. If an adult horse with diarrhoea is ill, particularly if they show signs of colic or have a raised temperature, consult your vet straightaway. With profuse diarrhoea a horse can become dehydrated very rapidly. You should look out for signs of dehydration (see page 77).

First Aid Treatment

❏ Stable the horse.

❏ Feed good hay, but no grass, and allow plenty of water to drink.

❏ Stop feeding concentrates and consider the use of probiotics, which may help some cases.

❏ As well as plain water, offer separate buckets of water with electrolytes.

❏ Check the horse's temperature. If it is elevated and the horse appears dehydrated and unwell, contact your vet.

❏ Look for oedema (accumulation of fluid) under the belly and on the lower limbs. This is a serious sign, and if you notice it, you should talk to your vet.

❏ Check your worming regime, as parasites can cause diarrhoea.

❏ There is always a small risk that diarrhoea can spread to other horses or people. For this reason it is sensible to be particularly careful with your own personal hygiene, and to keep the affected horse in, and away from other animals.

❏ Clean the dock area and buttocks, and apply petroleum jelly (Vaseline®) to reduce skin damage. It may be necessary to bandage the tail to keep it clean.

❏ Watch out for other problems such as laminitis that may develop.

Droppings from a yearling with worms: large round worms (white), tiny red worms (just visible)

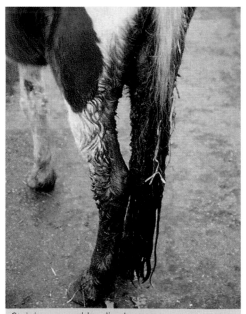

Staining caused by diarrhoea

Breathing Problems

Breathing difficulties can occur for several reasons, in particular the following:

1 Problems with the lungs taking in enough oxygen. The horse may be wheezing, coughing or breathing rapidly, and may have a sticky white/yellow discharge from the nose.

2 An obstruction somewhere in the airways, which prevents the air getting in or out of the lungs. Then the horse will make a loud respiratory noise, as if they are roaring or snoring.

Allergies

Most emergency breathing problems are associated with a dust allergy. People with asthma have breathless and wheezy attacks; similarly horses develop COPD (chronic obstructive pulmonary disease), also known as recurrent airway obstruction (RAO), broken wind, heaves or a stable cough. The worst cases will be perpetually breathless and/or coughing, with laboured breathing, heaving chest and flared nostrils (hence the name 'heaves'). Mild cases may just cough occasionally and have less stamina. These diseases develop as a result of an allergic response to organic dusts, particularly hay and straw dust, and associated fungal spores. Emergencies develop when a sensitized horse is exposed to excessive dust, for instance when stabled. To avoid problems, ensure adequate ventilation is maintained for stabled horses, especially in barns, and minimize dust by soaking hay and using dust-free bedding.

What to look out for
Contact a vet immediately in the following circumstances:

❑ The horse has rapidly become really breathless, and this does not improve within an hour. The horse should be placed in a dust-free, open, airy space – such as a paddock – and kept quiet and under close observation. Any exercise is liable to make breathlessness worse, so do not make the animal move unnecessarily.

❑ A breathless horse with a fever. This is uncommon, but it suggests an infection.

❑ There is severe persistent coughing, as the horse may have something stuck in his airways or gullet.

❑ The horse has recently suffered an injury to the chest.

❑ There is a new loud snoring/roaring sound all the time. If this noise is only present at exercise, it is not so urgent, but you should talk to your vet within the week if it persists.

What your vet will do
Your vet's treatment will depend on the suspected cause. Medicines can be prescribed that will rapidly help many breathing problems, although they may only control the signs temporarily rather than provide a cure. If there is an obstruction in the airway the vet may perform a tracheostomy (the insertion of a tube into the airway to allow the horse to breathe). In some cases your vet may recommend passing an endoscope, an instrument that allows them to examine the inside of the airways and lungs to find out what is wrong.

Infectious Respiratory Disease: Strangles

Some people will consider a horse with a dirty nose an emergency, especially if the discharge is like custard and the horse has swollen glands. There are many causes for such signs, particularly respiratory viral infections and dust allergies; yet inevitably there may be concern about strangles.

Respiratory infections, both bacterial and viral, can be very infectious, so early diagnosis and prompt action can reduce the spread of the disease.

Inevitably as horses move and mix together, all respiratory infections will spread, just like colds in people. Horses may be infectious yet show no signs, which is a good argument for quarantining any new arrival at a yard.

Key Facts about Strangles

❑ Strangles is a common bacterial infection in horses.

❑ Less than 1 per cent of infected horses will die of the disease.

❑ Only 2 to 7 per cent of horses will be affected by complications.

❑ The crucial concern is that it can spread from horse to horse, seriously curtailing equine activity.

❑ There is a need to act responsibly to limit the spread of the disease. This may mean keeping affected horses isolated/segregated for about 4 weeks after the disappearance of signs.

❑ You cannot tell if a horse definitely has strangles by clinical examination. Laboratory tests are required for clear confirmation, and more accurate tests are being developed all the time. It is important that you have an accurate diagnosis to be certain what you are dealing with, and to know whether strict isolation will be required.

How to Recognize Strangles

❑ A high temperature: at least 39–40°C or 102.5–104°F;

❑ depression and loss of appetite;

❑ a discharge from the nostrils;

❑ swollen glands;

❑ abscesses, usually in the throat region;

❑ occasionally a cough.

Some horses do not show all these signs, but have a mild atypical infection, which is often undetected.

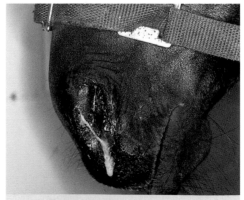

A horse with nasal discharge may have an infection or an allergy

How does Strangles Spread?

❑ Principally by direct contact from horse to horse – rubbing noses, sharing a drinking trough. It does not travel in the air for long distances, like foot and mouth virus.

❑ Poor hygiene amongst handlers: the infection is spread via clothes, buckets, tack and other contaminated kit.

❑ Even horses kept together do not always all contract the disease, in the same way that not all members of a family all catch the same cold.

❑ The strangles bug can linger for several weeks in the environment, so may persist in dirty stables, and particularly in dried-up puddles of pus and discharge. This illustrates the need to clean and disinfect thoroughly!

❑ Fortunately this infection is not airborne, so unlike foot and mouth disease, it will not spread long distances without some kind of direct contact.

❑ If the horses are isolated, care must still be taken to limit spread by indirect contact: for example, by people travelling from an infected yard to other horses. Strangles bugs will be killed by a hot (50°C) wash. A change of clothes and a shower should prevent indirect spread; however, it is best to avoid visiting an infected yard.

❑ If you are concerned that you may have a respiratory infection in the horses in your yard, contact your vet. The following precautionary measures will help:

❑ Take the horse's temperature regularly. A high temperature suggests infection.

❑ Keep any horses with suspicious signs of the disease away from other horses. Do not allow new animals to enter the yard unless they, too, can be kept in isolation.

❑ Take special care to ensure that infection is not spread through handlers, shared water troughs, direct contact or bedding and such like. Good hygiene and disinfection are important.

❑ Ensure your horses are properly vaccinated, particularly for equine flu.

❑ Seek veterinary attention if you suspect a contagious disease.

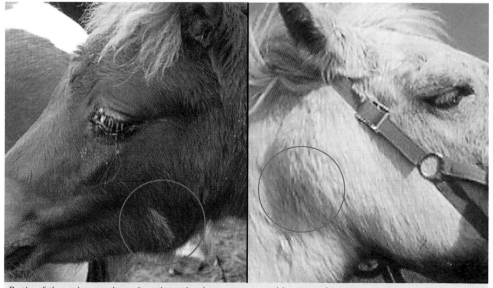

Both of these horses have lymph node abscesses caused by strangles

Choke

Choke is correctly called an 'oesophageal obstruction', and describes the situation where food becomes lodged within the gullet or oesophagus (the tube linking the mouth and stomach). Horses cannot vomit as we do, so become very distressed.

How to Recognize Choke

Often the signs are noticed immediately or soon after the horse has been fed. When a horse has choke, it is obvious that there is something wrong.

❑ Horses with choke are distressed, and will cough and splutter. Sometimes food and saliva pour from their mouth and nose as profuse green slime. Horses cannot vomit in the same way as people, but with acute choke they retch unpleasantly.

Other signs include:

❑ difficulty swallowing due to the obstruction;
❑ intermittent bending and stretching of the neck in an attempt to shift the blockage;
❑ there may be a visible swelling or a lump to be felt on the left side of the neck;

❑ initially an affected horse may still try to eat, even though the food passage is blocked. If the blockage does not shift, they lose their appetite and become dehydrated.

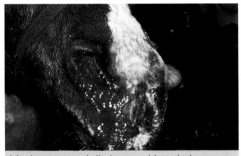
Unpleasant nasal discharge with a choke case

What To Do

Choke looks like a dire emergency, but it usually isn't! Most cases resolve rapidly without treatment and do not justify veterinary attention. However, the risk of complications increases significantly the longer the duration of the obstruction. The biggest risk is the horse inhaling food and saliva, and then developing pneumonia as a complication. Some aspiration pneumonia is seen in about two thirds of cases. If the obstruction does not shift within a few hours, you will need veterinary help. First aid:

❑ Prevent the horse from eating or drinking anything further, so he is less likely to get food down the windpipe. It is best to put them in a box with no hay or water and with non-edible bedding, and then contact your vet for advice. By the time you have done so, the obstruction will frequently have cleared.

❑ Occasionally a lump of obstructed food can be felt on the left side of the neck, and massaging this gently may help it to disperse.

❑ Keep the horse quiet, with their head low to allow saliva to drain. The vet may give them a sedative to encourage this.

What Your Vet will Do

The vet's management of the situation depends on how long the choke has been going on, and how uncomfortable the horse is. The majority will simply need injections to relax them and allow the obstruction to pass. If the choke persists, the vet may use more aggressive treatment. Sometimes a stomach tube is passed up the nose into the oesophagus to confirm the site of the obstruction, and fluid may be gently pumped through to soften and shift the blockage. Giving large amounts of fluids as an intravenous drip will help, as the horse can become dehydrated through continually dribbling saliva and being unable to drink. On rare occasions a general anaesthetic is needed to shift a blockage using various surgical procedures.

The prognosis for a complete recovery after one episode of choke is good. Withholding dry fibrous foods for at least three days can reduce the chance of recurrence or scarring at the site of the obstruction. Any associated respiratory infections will usually rapidly resolve, but many choke cases need antibiotics for a few days.

Causes of Choke

❑ Choke is usually caused by dry feed swelling as saliva combines with it, to block the oesophagus; inadequately soaked sugar beet is the classic cause, and the obstruction is made worse by further food that piles up behind the blockage. Other substances that may also cause choke include pieces of fruit or vegetables, chunks of wood, or even shavings.

❑ An often underestimated reason for choke is feeding a horse too soon after they have recovered from sedation or anaesthesia; so be patient, and give your horse time to wake up before giving them the equine equivalent of tea and biscuits! Another potential risk is the exhausted horse; so ensure they drink before they eat, and that all feed is sloppy and easy to swallow.

❑ If a horse has repeated bouts of choke, it is worth looking for an underlying cause. Once feeding problems can be ruled out, it is important to consider other possible causes:
  • Dental difficulties: sharp or worn teeth in older horses, and loose or erupting teeth in younger ones.
  • Very occasionally some kind of obstruction pressing on the outside of the oesophagus can prevent the smooth passage of food. This can include neck injuries that cause swelling, including abscesses such as those associated with strangles, and more unusually, tumours.
  • Other conditions that cause difficulty swallowing have to be considered. In some areas of the world this includes serious conditions such as rabies, which can mimic choke.
  • Greed: there are certainly horses – and ponies in particular – who just gobble their food and get it stuck, but have nothing medically wrong.

Preventing Choke
❑ Avoid dry feed.
❑ Feed the horse away from others so they do not rush when they eat because of the fear of another horse snatching their supper.
❑ Try feeding a smaller amount at a higher frequency so that the horse gets the same amount of feed per day as it was previously, but in three or four lots.
❑ Put a large object that is too big to eat, such as a large stone, in the feed bowl so that the horse has to search for their feed and so eat more slowly.

Muscle Problems

Tying up, set-fast, azoturia and 'Monday morning disease' are all traditional names used to describe a horse suffering from a muscle disorder. More technically, this is known as paralytic myoglobinuria, myositis, or most properly, exertional rhabdomyolysis syndrome (ERS). Such names describe the condition, but not the cause. Tying up and set-fast describe a horse that cannot move. Myositis and rhabdomyolysis describe the muscle damage involved. Azoturia and myoglobinuria describe how the damaged muscles result in discoloured urine. Monday morning disease describes the historic problem when draft horses were fed normal rations on Sunday, but were left in and not worked, so they subsequently seized up on Monday!

Not only are there many different names, there are also many different disorders, with multiple causes; hence it can be a confusing emergency. In the past it was thought that your horse 'tied up' or developed some kind of muscle cramp because you had got the feeding wrong; now it is known that the causes are a lot more complicated. Recent research has shown that in some cases it is inherited, and because there are many different causes, there is no one magic cure.

Two collapsed horses on drips being nursed in a padded box. Both animals are suffering from a muscle disorder called atypical myoglobinuria

Signs to Look For

❑ Muscle damage

There will be stiffness and reluctance to move; sometimes the horse will completely seize up, and on rare occasions can even become recumbent. Discoloured (red-brown) urine can be passed as a result of muscle breakdown products being passed out through the kidneys

❑ Pain

Depending on the horse and the severity of muscle damage, they will be very uncomfortable. Signs include sweating, pawing the ground, and raised pulse and respiratory rates. They are sensitive on muscle palpation, particularly around the powerful rump, thigh and back muscles. They can be so distressed that the condition may be confused with colic. The mild cases are more difficult to identify, and can be confused with low-grade lameness.

Pulled Muscles

Remember that horses can pull muscles and be stiff after unaccustomed exercise, especially if they are unfit. Nevertheless, it is best to consult a vet in order to rule out other potential causes of such lameness, as many cases of suspected muscle strain actually have other causes. A true muscle strain will benefit from rest and/or manipulation.

❑ Associated electrolyte and fluid imbalances

This affliction often happens whilst the horse is working, when there already is a degree of dehydration and electrolyte loss. Sweating makes this worse, and in a dehydrated horse, muscle breakdown products can damage the kidneys. This can result in kidney failure.

Horse in sling following muscle damage

What To Do

Immediate action

❑ Stop exercise, and if you are some distance from home, it is generally advisable to box back, as long as the horse is fit to travel, rather than ride.

❑ If it is cold, rug the horse up.

❑ If the horse is in pain, or is sweating dramatically, call your vet immediately.

❑ Stable the horse and give him hay and water, but no concentrates.

Subsequent preventive measures

❑ Ensure the diet contains as much forage as possible, either from pasture, hay, or hay equivalents. This provides essential fibre and should be 50 per cent of the diet; if practical, forage alone is often ideal. Any supplementary feed needs to be high in fibre and low in energy. This means that only a small amount of cereals (which are high in starch) should be fed, or none at all. There are specially developed high fat, low starch feeds appropriate for such horses. Also, the gradual introduction of oil is frequently recommended; oil can be fed as vegetable oil such as corn oil or soya oil. It is best to obtain specific veterinary and nutritionist advice as to what is appropriate for a particular case, especially as some high oil diets will require extra vitamins and electrolytes.

❏ Avoid box rest and ensure the high-risk horse has daily turnout on sparse grazing for as long as possible.

❏ Ensure that horses are not cold whilst they are turned out, so provide shelter and rugs as required.

❏ If you feed concentrates, feed as little as you can of a low energy feed, and only increase the feed once the horse's work has increased.

❏ Most cases benefit from a long, slow warm-up and a gradual cool-down after exercise.

❏ Reduce work if there is evidence of any respiratory viral infections in the vicinity.

❏ Some horses, particularly mares, are thought to be more prone to muscle disease when they feel stressed, so keep stressful situations to a minimum in any way you can.

❏ Keep to a regular, consistent routine as regards daily exercise and turnout and feeding.

Muscles can take some weeks to repair, and the vet is likely to monitor progress by blood tests. It is most important that the horse does not return to work too soon.

Identifying the Trigger Factor

Many horses that suffer from 'tying up' (exertional rhabdomyolysis syndrome, or ERS) have an underlying tendency to develop the condition, which is then triggered by one or more factors, one of which is usually exercise. The difficulty is identifying the trigger factors, since very often what will prevent tying up in one horse will have no effect on another. There are often links with diet, fitness and exercise.

In America, two specific categories of sufferer have been discovered, though the causes of their disorder are quite different:

❏ Certain lines of thoroughbred horses (about 5 per cent), which tend to suffer from recurrent tying up due to a disorder in muscle contractility. This is an inherited problem.

❏ Another totally different but also inherited muscle disorder, seen particularly in quarter horses, warmbloods and draft breeds, and known as polysaccharide storage myopathy (PSSM); it is linked with abnormal energy storage in muscle tissue. An alarming point is that a case is not always detectable using the blood tests routinely undertaken by vets in tying up cases; instead, muscle biopsies are required to make a definite diagnosis. The good news is that in a lot of cases the disorder can be effectively controlled by feeding a high fat, high fibre, low starch/sugar diet plus careful management

Eye Injuries

If your horse is keeping one eye partially or completely closed, it means it hurts. Infections, inflammation or foreign bodies in the eye can all cause pain, and other reactions including reddening of the membranes around the eye, and a discharge from the eye itself. Horse owners are accustomed to seeing a slight discharge, particularly associated with flies in summer and dusty stables in winter, so sometimes a more significant discharge is overlooked.

A painful eye should never be ignored: eyes are irreplaceable, so it is not worth taking any risks concerning their welfare, particularly as certain conditions can deteriorate very rapidly; for instance, 'melting ulcers' start with a weepy eye, but then rapidly result in catastrophic loss of vision due to sudden severe infection. An unusually runny eye should therefore always be checked by a vet.

Painful, shut eye showing water and discharge which is an emergency

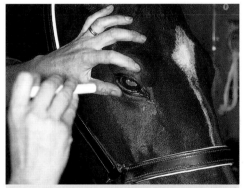

Vet checking eye using a bright light

First Aid Management

Various steps can be taken to make the horse more comfortable; however, any eye injury will nearly always need veterinary attention. In the event of injury, you could follow the procedures that are described below:

❏ Wipe away any discharge to deter flies. The application of petroleum jelly (Vaseline®) to the face around the eye may help reduce scalding of the skin.

❏ If an irritant chemical is splashed into the eye, then flushing it with clean water is justified. However, consult a vet before using anything else in the eye, and never introduce any product into the injured eye in an attempt to neutralize the offending agent, as it is more likely to cause further irritation.

❏ The irritation and discomfort from an eye problem will often drive a horse to rub their eye, making things worse. One of the best ways of preventing this is to use a pair of blinkers as protection; meanwhile in an emergency, just hold a horse to prevent him rubbing whilst professional help is sought. If the horse is well behaved, an ice pack (frozen peas

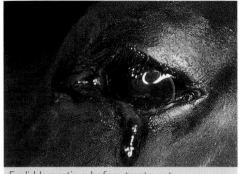

Eyelid laceration: before treatment

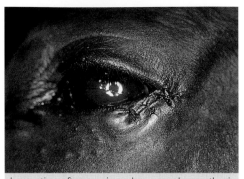

Laceration after repair under general anaesthesia

would do!) in between layers of soft clean cloth held against the eye for five minutes may help to soothe it.

❑ If the eye is weeping and you can see the surface of the eyeball, look for a foggy or cloudy area on the front of the eye: this may be an ulcer needing urgent veterinary attention. Also look for foreign bodies or blood in or around the eye, and if you see either, call your vet.

❑ Never try to force the eyelids open if the eye is shut, as this can damage it even further. It is far better to allow your vet to do this by using appropriate painkillers.

❑ If there is anything protruding from the eye, never remove it: what you see sticking out may be a part of the inside of the eye itself, which is plugging a wound that has perforated the front of the eye. Pulling out a foreign body such as a long hair or piece of straw could slice through the surface of the eye. Gently bathe around the eye if you can do so without causing discomfort. Boiled and cooled water is best in an emergency.

❑ Many horses with eye problems are sensitive to light, and they may feel better if placed in a quiet, dark stable free of dust and flies.

❑ Feeding on the floor will help avoid the problem of dust dropping from a haynet or manger, and thus further irritating an already sore eye.

❑ If the eyelid edge sustains a wound, your vet should repair it as soon as possible to avoid later complications. A general anaesthetic may be needed to perform a proper repair; if it is left to heal itself there may be serious scarring and damage to the eye.

Safety Note

Eye ointments deteriorate over time, so should never be kept for longer than their 'sell-by' date. What is ideal for treating one eye condition could make another worse! Always consult your vet.

Emergency Skin Problems

Urticaria (Nettle Rash or Hives)

Multiple raised lumps swell up all over the skin, often starting small and coalescing into larger masses, and the sight of this may well produce concern. The rash may affect the whole body, or just one area. It looks very like the sort of rash that appears if you touch a clump of nettles, and indeed this may be the cause for some horses that have been unfortunate enough to roll in nettles.

Certainly the cause will be some kind of allergy, but often it is not as obvious as the skin reaction to field nettles, and frequently will remain a mystery: it could be anything with which the horse has had contact, such as pollens, washes or fly repellents, feeds or feed supplements.

Some thin-skinned animals, particularly thoroughbreds, may be quite distressed if they have rolled in stinging nettles. They may try to roll to relieve the itching, and be very wobbly on their legs due to the discomfort: so be aware that something that looks serious might just be nettle rash.

Many cases will clear up without treatment; however, you ought to contact your vet in the following circumstances:
- ❏ if the horse is uncomfortable and seems unwell;
- ❏ if there is any problem with their breathing;
- ❏ if the skin around the eyes and nose is very swollen;
- ❏ if the rash does not subside in 24 hours.

In treating such sudden allergic reations, vets often recommend steroids to control the inflammation, together with removal of the cause, if it can be identified. In some cases such as pregnant mares or likely laminitis sufferers, steroids cannot be used safely. Sometimes antihistamines are used instead. In some cases the lumps may persist or recur.

Urticaria: skin lumps like a nettle rash

Ringworm

Sometimes urticaria is confused with the early stages of this common infectious fungal skin infection. However, although ringworm is never fatal and is not a genuine emergency, the concern is to recognize the condition and to limit its spread. Ringworm can appear in many different disguises. If in doubt, any skin rash, or sore or bald area should be checked for ringworm. This is one condition where treatment may be justifiable – just in case – in order to limit spread. Ringworm can affect horses and humans.

How to recognize ringworm
- ❑ The fungus grows across the surface of the skin and around the hairs, producing a variety of changes affecting a horse's coat and skin.
- ❑ Initially tufts of hair may appear raised, with a slight swelling underneath like nettle rash.

Where to Find Ringworm
- ❑ On horses it is most often found where the tack rubs the skin.
- ❑ Young horses have less immunity and are more susceptible.
- ❑ Crowded stable yards always put horses at greater risk of infection, especially in cool, damp weather.

- ❑ The ringworm may produce gray, flaking circular patches with broken hairs, though it is more likely to be any shape.
- ❑ The skin then looks raw and sore as tufts of hair fall out, leaving bald patches.
- ❑ The coat will then regrow, however hair loss is a typical symptom.

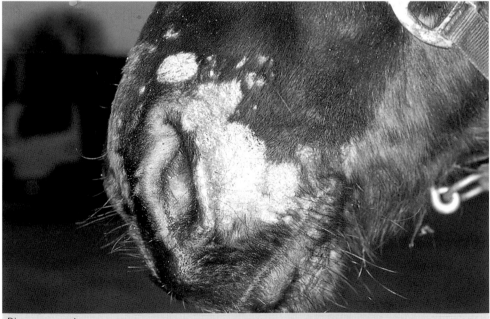

Ringworm rash

What to do about ringworm

- ❏ Keep the horse isolated in his own box, ensuring that he cannot touch other horses.
- ❏ Do not groom or clip an affected horse because of the risk of spreading spores.
- ❏ Avoid riding an affected horse to reduce the chance of spread, and to prevent skin sores being rubbed by tack.
- ❏ Do not share rugs, tack or grooming kit.
- ❏ Ask your vet to check any suspected case. It is possible that they can diagnose it from the visible signs, but lab tests may also be needed.
- ❏ Ringworm is one of the few conditions you can catch from your horse. If your horse has a skin irritation and you develop a rash, you should seek medical advice.

How ringworm spreads

Ringworm spreads either by direct contact or on grooming kit or tack, buckets or rugs. The ringworm fungus produces spores, which can remain dormant on woodwork for over a year. Stables and fencing can become contaminated, explaining why some horses develop ringworm when put in a previously empty stable. It is best not to share tack at all, particularly girths which, when damp and sweaty, create an ideal way for ringworm to spread.

The usual incubation period for ringworm is between one and four weeks. However most cases, if left, will eventually clear up on their own, nevertheless they are best treated to avoid further spread and contamination of the environment.

Controlling Ringworm

The aim is firstly to kill the fungus, usually with medicated washes; and secondly to destroy the spores, reducing environmental contamination. Stables should be thoroughly cleaned and dirty bedding destroyed. Disinfect the rugs, fences and anything else in contact with a case. Some yards do nothing – and even allow horses to mix in so-called 'ringworm parties' – as the infection is self-limiting, but this is not ideal because although horses may become immune, it will only be to that one strain.

Bites and Stings

These are a possible emergency, which can cause swelling of the affected part, usually the muzzle or limb. Snake bites can cause severe swelling, particularly on a horse's nose, and this may cause a respiratory obstruction.

This is more likely to be a problem in a hot climate. In the USA, the bite of the black widow spider can cause a hot, painful swelling, as can that of the fire ant, prevalent in the south-eastern United States. Bee stings are more common, and can be identified by the circular area of oedema, usually with the sting visible in the centre of the swelling; try and pull out the sting.

Deal with this sort of emergency in the following way:

- ❏ Apply cold treatment to reduce swelling.
- ❏ Remove any obvious bee sting if it is possible to do so easily. Sodium bicarbonate may soothe bee stings, and vinegar for wasps
- ❏ If there is extensive swelling, contact a vet who may administer anti-inflammatory and pain-killing medication.
- ❏ Because of the size of the patient, plus the risk of adverse reactions and the usual time delay between the bite and realizing what has happened, antivenom is rarely used for snake bite.

Tetanus

Toxins produced by tetanus bacteria cause the deadly disease tetanus. The bugs are commonly present in soil and easily infect wounds: they can enter the body anywhere if the outer defence layer of hoof, skin or membranes has been damaged. In many cases this is through a tiny puncture wound that the owner never notices. Routine vaccination will totally prevent the disease and is strongly recommended for all horses and their owners. Horses are particularly susceptible to this unpleasant infection, which causes serious and traumatic suffering and is usually fatal.

Signs of Tetanus

After a one- to four-week incubation period, the toxins produced by the tetanus bug will reach the brain, causing confusing signals to be sent out to muscles. The following signs are typical of this disease:

❑ The ability to eat and drink becomes increasingly difficult as the jaw muscles lock (lockjaw).
❑ All movement is restricted as the muscles go into spasm: initially this starts simply as a stiff gait, but at the end the horse becomes recumbent.

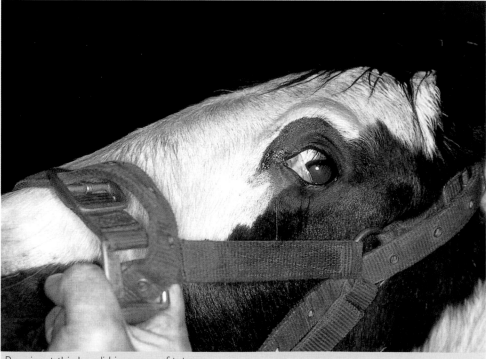

Prominent third eyelid in a case of tetanus.

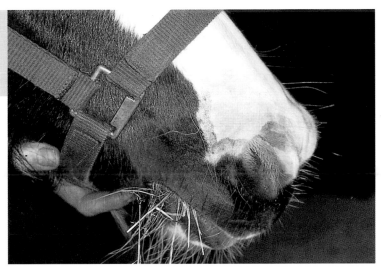

Foal with tetanus with food stuck in his mouth as he is unable to swallow

❏ Food and water are regurgitated through the nostrils, as the muscles involved with chewing and swallowing fail.

❏ A nasty 'smirk' is assumed on the face where the lip muscles are drawn back.

❏ The third eyelid is seen more prominently as a white triangle over the eyeball (see left).

❏ Any stimulus, particularly a loud noise, causes worsening signs.

❏ Horses frequently die in convulsions or as a result of paralysis of the respiratory muscles. It is an unpleasant death, and no one who has seen a horse with this illness ever wants to repeat the experience, and will vaccinate everything.

What To Do

The obvious answer is to avoid the infection by having yourself, and your horses and ponies vaccinated. The vaccine is very safe and effective, it is inexpensive, and once the initial vaccine course has been given it only requires a booster every two or three years depending on your vet's advice and the incidence of tetanus in your area.

If you notice that your horse has a wound and he is not vaccinated, your vet can administer a tetanus antitoxin that will provide short-term immediate protection against any tetanus infection. This is not a true vaccination, however, and it is best to start a course of vaccination as well. Cleaning any wound properly will reduce the risk of exposure to tetanus.

The fact that tetanus has an incubation period of at least a week means that protecting a horse with an injury that is not vaccinated is not a middle-of-the-night emergency. However, you should still contact your vet the following day.

Of all diseases, this is the one that is cheaply and easily prevented, but costly, traumatic and often futile to attempt to cure.

Prognosis

If the horse can still drink and stand, the chance of recovery is fair, with good nursing care. However, once an equine tetanus case is recumbent, more than 75 per cent of cases will die. Note that recovery from tetanus does not protect against the disease, and any equine tetanus survivor still needs to be vaccinated regularly.

Nosebleeds

Nosebleeds (properly known as 'epistaxis') in horses are often due to a blow on the head. A slight bleed from one nostril – less than enough to fill a teacup, and which stops within 15 minutes – is unlikely to be serious, but do seek veterinary advice if it should happen again.

A moderate nosebleed, if accompanied by coughing, suggests that a foreign body is wedged in the nose or throat. This, or a copious nosebleed, is a true emergency, and the vet should be contacted immediately, particularly if the horse is distressed.

Mild nosebleed

Cause of Nosebleeds

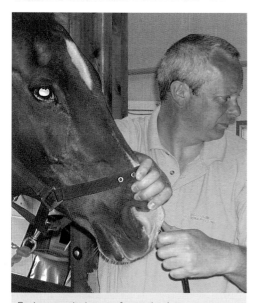

Endoscopy being performed using a videoendoscope. The tube is threaded up the horse's nose, and the image is examined by the vet on a TV monitor

❑ The cause of a small, one-off nosebleed may never be found, but with recurrent or persistent nosebleeds, the vet may suggest endoscopy (an examination of the internal structures with a flexible instrument that enables them to see what is going on inside).

❑ X-ray pictures may also be required to detect skull damage.

❑ To investigate a horse with a serious nosebleed properly, a referral may be required to an equine hospital with the facilities and expertise to operate if necessary.

❑ There are some rare, but serious equine conditions that start as tiny nosebleeds, then worsen (particularly guttural pouch mycosis); so always get a significant or recurrent nosebleed checked out promptly.

❑ A hospital investigation does not necessarily mean that major surgery is required, however ultimately it is the best place to go for a diagnosis and cure.

What To Do

- With any nosebleed, the horse should be kept as calm as possible.
- The nose should never be packed, as horses breathe through their noses, so this would only make the situation worse.
- If the bleeding is coming from inside the nose area, it may help to hold an ice pack or cold wet towel just below the horse's eyes.
- Remember that horses are big animals and their body contains a lot of blood, so what looks like a significant nosebleed, may not be critical. Even so, a nosebleed should not continue for more than 15 minutes; if it does, consult the vet urgently. If possible, advise the vet whether the bleed is from one nostril, which means it is coming from inside the nose area, or from both nostrils, which suggests it originates somewhere further back.

Headshaking

In reality this is rarely going to be an immediate emergency crisis; however, if your horse does suddenly start to headshake, it can be disconcerting to say the least.

Headshaking can have many possible causes, not all of which are understood. However, if a horse suddenly starts to headshake violently it is worth considering some sort of insect bite or sting, as well as a possible foreign body caught somewhere – for instance, in the nose; however, these are unlikely to be the true cause. The majority of headshaking cases are now shown to be due to nerve irritation, sometimes stimulated by influences such as bright light, pollens, or a previous viral infection, that can cause a degree of pain or irritation elsewhere.

What To Do

- Stop riding: most horses do not exhibit headshaking behaviour when at rest in the stable or at grass, but signs generally begin once the animal has warmed up at exercise.
- Ride with a nose net designed to stop headshaking. There are several such products on the market now, some of which help some cases.
- Try to ride at a different time of day or in a different area, where whatever stimulates the irritation is not present.
- If the headshaking persists, you should consult your vet. Unfortunately it is difficult to find both cause and cure in many cases.

Nose net designed to stop headshaking

Heat Stroke

Heat stroke associated with over-exertion is a major issue in hot, humid countries, and it should not be overlooked in the UK, either, particularly in unfit, overweight horses, or those carrying a thick coat. As a horse sweats, he loses mostly water and electrolytes, or body salts as they are frequently called. If both these constituents are lost and not replaced, a horse will become dehydrated and his performance will be affected. If a rider does not detect the early signs of fatigue in their horse and stop, more major problems can result, such as 'thumps', muscle disorders and heat stroke.

Giving electrolytes to an endurance horse

Thumps

This condition is properly called 'asynchronous diaphragmatic flutter'. It is a little like hiccups, in that the horse's flank twitches and makes an audible thump: hence the name. It is most commonly seen in horses doing endurance rides, and indicates that an electrolyte disturbance is present. Appropriate intra-venous veterinary treatment to correct the metabolic imbalance should quickly return everything to normal.

Muscle Disorders

More seriously, electrolyte disturbances can result in muscle disorders such as tying up or azoturia, when the horse will look stiff and be reluctant to move, and may completely seize up.

Heat Stroke

Heat stroke is when the horse overheats, and his own body-cooling systems are overloaded and cannot cool him down. If not caught early, this can lead to the alarming combination of heat stroke and dehydration, known as **exhausted horse syndrome**.

All these conditions are potentially serious, and the affected horse will benefit from rapid aggres-sive treatment, so it is highly advisable to

❑ seek immediate veterinary help; and
❑ try to prevent the horse becoming over-heated, overtired or dehydrated.

Prevention

Ensure the horse drinks

Generally a horse will drink more water than he needs. Exactly how much water an individual horse will drink per day depends on the moisture content of the feed he eats, the work he is doing, and the day-to-day climatic conditions. In hot, humid conditions a horse will need to increase his water intake at least fourfold, hence dehydration is a risk.

Recognize dehydration

Relatively low levels of dehydration can affect performance. Traditionally, dehydration is checked by gently pinching a couple of centimetres of skin over the shoulder between finger and thumb, then releasing it; in a healthy horse, theoretically it rapidly pings back into place. In reality even normal horses can have a small crease of skin persisting longer than might be expected. A horse has to be seriously dehydrated for a skin pinch test to be obviously positive.

A skin pinch test for dehydration can be misleading

Performance may therefore be affected below the level that a skin pinch test would detect, so it should not be relied on without assessing other signs; these might include dry or tacky gums, and in severe cases a weak, fast pulse, sunken eyes, and cool extremities.

It may not be that obvious that there is a problem, especially when dehydrated horses have been shown to sweat less than normal animals.

Replace fluid and electrolytes at every opportunity

Allow frequent small drinks when exercising, and do not withhold water before competing. Naturally water and electrolytes will be replenished by a horse's normal diet, but there may not be the opportunity to do so when competing. Rapid rehydration with water alone will just dilute the body fluids and further disturb the electrolyte balance. It is now known that electrolytes, and particularly sodium, are also needed, if water alone is given.

This is well recognized by human athletes, hence the large market for special sports drinks. Equine athletes benefit from the same sort of thing, and a variety of equine oral replacement electrolyte solutions is available commercially. It is important that they are made up at the correct concentration, and that the horse will take them.

There is always a chance that by adding electrolytes

When to Give Electrolytes

It is impossible for a horse to store extra electrolytes for future needs, so there is little point in giving extra electrolytes on a regular basis, except to get him accustomed to the taste! If there are potential concerns, it may be sensible to give some just before a competition to ensure the horse is fully hydrated before it starts.

Under normal conditions an adult horse on a good diet will receive sufficient electrolytes, in particular from good quality forage, and also from the trace-mineralized salt in top quality, commercially prepared, equine concentrate mixes. Horses that sweat excessively may need additional salt added, at approximately 1 per cent of their daily ration. It is usually sufficient to give an electrolyte supplement with which the horse's tastebuds are familiar as soon as possible after major exertion with sweating.

to drinking water the horse will not drink it. Professionals sometimes add apple squash or apple juice to mask the taste; apple sauce also works quite well for making a paste. If horses are trained to this before a competition they usually accept it when they need salt supplementation.

Cooling the Horse

Any horse with a very high temperature needs to be cooled down.

- ❑ Start by removing any extra rugs.
- ❑ If a horse has a really high temperature in hot weather, it will help to bathe him with a sponge soaked in cool, but not cold water. Concentrate on the areas behind and between the ears, the forehead, the underside of the neck where the jugular vein lies, the girth and dock. Avoid running ice-cold water (such as with a hose) over the back and quarters for long periods, as this can reduce blood flow to these muscle masses and so increase heating in the body core.
- ❑ Ensure that the hot horse stands in the shade, ideally where there is a breeze, or use a fan.

Cooling a horse

Avoiding Heat Stroke

Although heat stroke is mostly a problem for competition horses, it can affect any horse.

❑ Remember weather forecasts quote the temperature in the shade, so a horse out in a field with no shade or shelter and a limited water supply can also suffer, particularly if he is dark coloured and/or overweight, as they absorb heat more easily.

❑ Horses being transported or left standing in horseboxes, or even worse, trailers, suffer enormously, especially if deprived of water as well.

❑ At home, do not leave your horse shut in a hot, stuffy stable on oppressive days when there is no breeze at all.

You Can Take a Horse to Water...

A horse should always be encouraged to drink. When travelling, soaked hay and sloppy wet feeds are the easiest way to get water on board.

Paradoxically thirst may be suppressed in the exhausted, dehydrated horse. If they will not drink, then a vet can administer fluids using a stomach tube. This is passed up the nose, swallowed, and then directed down towards the stomach, and can be a useful way of replacing both water and electrolytes rapidly. However, it can be difficult to pass a stomach tube in an exhausted, dehydrated horse, and often results in a nosebleed. In a very sick horse the fluid may just pool in the gut, so intravenous fluids may be a better option.

Very sick or severely dehydrated horses require fluids given directly into the blood circulation via a sterile catheter usually placed in the main jugular vein in the neck (right). Large volumes of fluid and electrolytes can be given in this way. There are ready-made 5-litre packs of fluid, ten times the volume of the little drip sets given to most sick people in hospital. In people the fluid is dripped in slowly, but with horses large volumes of fluid are run in rapidly, sometimes upwards of 80 litres being given in a single day. Intravenous fluids can be a lifesaver for many dehydrated horses.

Foaling

Most foals arrive naturally without the need for any intervention. The incidence of difficult births – dystocia – in the mare is low (less than 4 per cent), but if things do go wrong, prompt effective assistance is vital. Having an experienced attendant watching the mare and then assisting if necessary is the best way to reduce the risk of problems at foaling. If you are inexperienced, it is difficult to know what is normal and when you need to worry. Therefore owners who are uncertain about midwifery for their mare should send her away so she can foal in experienced hands, or should arrange to have someone experienced on hand.

When Will the Foal Arrive?

The simple answer is, not when expected! Mares rarely foal when predicted, and may need checking for weeks before anything happens. The average length of gestation in the mare is 342 days, but it can easily range from 320 to 365 days. A useful guide to remember is 11 months and 4 days, but some mares have been known to carry their foal for longer, with minimal ill effects.

Pre-Foaling Emergencies

❏ The crisis most likely to cause concern is if your pregnant mare loses her foal. Surprisingly, in most cases the mare is remarkably unbothered, and it is the owner who is distressed and uncertain what to do. The best approach is to check to see if the mare has lost one or two foals. Twins are one reason why an equine pregnancy fails. Twins usually results in abortion at 7 to 8 months, or undersized live or dead foals are at term. The reason for the low survival rate of twins is due to competition for placental space.

❏ Isolate the mare that has lost her foal, and prevent other pregnant mares from coming into contact with the area; certainly keep them away from the dead foal and placenta. This is important because there are infectious agents (particularly equine herpes virus) that can spread to other pregnant mares, causing them to lose their foals as well.

❏ Contact a vet, as it is useful to establish the cause of abortion where possible, and so plan appropriate preventive measures.

Preparation for Foaling

Mares should be well cared for during pregnancy to optimize the likelihood of a healthy foal. A sensible management programme would include:
   ❏ adequate but not excessive feeding;
   ❏ proper parasite control;
   ❏ vaccinating the mare before foaling to ensure that her colostrum has the necessary antibodies;
   ❏ moving the mare to the place where she is going to foal six weeks before she is due; this will accustom her to the new environment and routine, and will also ensure that her colostrum contains the necessary antibodies to protect the foal against local infections.

Foaling Facilities

Ideally mares should foal in a special foaling box – at least 3 × 3m for an average Thoroughbred mare – and well ventilated, but free from draughts. Bedding should be dust free, preferably of high quality straw, and plenty of it. It needs to be located somewhere convenient for easy, unobtrusive night-time checking. Some form of low-level lighting that can be left on all night is preferable to constantly switching the main stable lights on and off. A basic first-aid kit should be available for every foaling, and should include:

- ❏ a tail bandage for the mare;
- ❏ clean buckets and towels;
- ❏ a suitable antiseptic, for example pevidine;
- ❏ sterile scissors.

Kit can be sterilized by boiling, then stored in clean, sealed plastic bags.

Also consider in advance if there is any available milk source, should it be needed. Many equine vets and some studs keep emergency supplies of spare colostrum and replacement mare's milk for foals, and it is worth establishing the whereabouts of such supplies, just in case.

Monitoring the Mare for Foaling

Keep the mare under close observation late in pregnancy, and as she approaches her foaling date, but without disturbing her. Certain physical changes will indicate impending delivery:

- ❏ The udder or mammary gland will develop. It increases in size during the last month of pregnancy, and changes are particularly noticeable in the two weeks before birth.
- ❏ The pelvic ligaments will relax.
- ❏ The vulva will lengthen.
- ❏ Just before foaling the udder typically becomes very swollen, and there is a waxy secretion on the teat ends; this is known as 'waxing' and is usually a sign that foaling will happen within one to four days. Sometimes milk can run from the udder ahead of foaling, and if too much of the first milk – colostrum – is lost, the foal can be left short and therefore put at risk. In this case they must be given extra colostrum, either dried or a pre-frozen natural supply, and special care in their first few days of life.

Mares vary tremendously in the signs they actually show; some appear normal, and the first their owners know about the foal is when they suddenly find him with the mare! To avoid having to check the mare repeatedly and in person, and potentially over many weeks, there are various time-saving options:

- ❏ It is possible to measure the electrolyte concentrations in pre-foaling udder secretions using kits that are available commercially. When the amount of calcium in the milk increases above a certain level, over 95 per cent of mares will foal within 72 hours.
- ❏ Various foaling alarm systems are available, such as a small transmitter lightly stitched to the mare's vulva; when she pushes the foetal membranes through the vulva, the alarm is triggered. The disadvantage is that the alarm only sounds once the mare actually starts to deliver, so the attendant needs to be nearby.
- ❏ Other foaling alarm systems strap around the whole mare and sound an alarm if or when she sweats during delivery. The disadvantage of these is that if the mare does not sweat it does not go off.
- ❏ Close-circuit TV is also commonly used, but as delivery is very rapid in the mare (sometimes fifteen minutes or less), it is important to watch closely. If disturbed they are unlikely to proceed. Most mares foal at night because they prefer a quiet environment.

The Three Stages of Foaling Down

Foaling is a continuous process, but for easier reference it is usual to divide it into three stages.

THE FIRST STAGE

This lasts from one to four hours, and begins with the onset of contractions. During this stage the foal begins to move of his own accord, rotating himself and extending the front legs and head. Mares do not normally strain during the first stage, but they do show discomfort and other signs, including:

- ❑ becoming restless and showing colic-like signs (looking at the flanks, tail switching, frequently getting up and down);
- ❑ patchy sweating (flanks, neck, behind elbows);
- ❑ yawning.

At the end of first stage labour the cervix is fully dilated; at this stage the membranes rupture, and several litres of fluid escape (popularly called 'the waters breaking'). As the mare approaches the end of first stage labour, her tail should be bandaged and her vulval area cleaned and dried.

THE SECOND STAGE

The onset of the second stage is abrupt, with the mare starting forcible abdominal straining, and/or the appearance of the membranes that surround the foal. The mare now usually lies down on her side until the foal is born; it should take less than 25 minutes from the waters breaking to the birth of the foal.

- ❑ The outer placental membrane ruptures, and the amnion (the transparent bluish-white

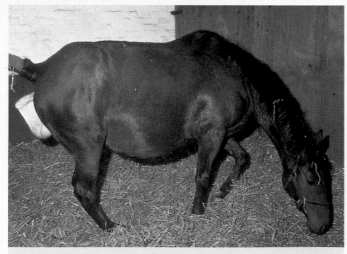

FOALING: 1. Start of second stage and appearance of membranes as mare lies down

FOALING: 2. Both front feet and normal presentation

membrane) should soon be visible at the vulva. Fluid and a foetal foot should be obvious. Regular contractions should continue, then both front feet should appear, usually with one foreleg in front of the other by some 10cm. The nose should emerge shortly afterwards.

❑ The greatest effort is associated with delivering the head, then the passage of the chest and hips usually occurs relatively easily. As the head and shoulders pass through the pelvis, the amnion should rupture. If necessary, the mare can be assisted by gentle pulling on the foal's front legs. Sometimes it helps to break the membranes so the foal can breathe.

❑ The foal has a relatively long umbilical cord, which is still intact after delivery. If possible, the cord should be left intact for a few minutes to help the circulation in the newborn foal. Care should be taken not to disturb the mare at this stage, or she may get up and rupture the cord. The cord usually ruptures at a predetermined place, dictated by the movements of the mare and/or foal several minutes (up to 15 minutes) after birth.

❑ Once the umbilical cord has ruptured, the stump should be checked for haemorrhage, and disinfected with dilute chlorhexidine (Hibiscrub®). The cord is rarely tied, as this encourages infection. The navel needs to be disinfected several times during the first few days of life. If the mare is still lying down, the foal can be moved towards her head to try and reduce the risk of being trampled on when she stands up. All disturbances should be kept to a minimum during this stage.

THE THIRD STAGE

This involves the passage of the foetal membranes or placenta, often termed 'delivery of the afterbirth'; it should not take more than three hours.

nose visible within membranes,

FOALING: 3. Membranes broken by foal's movements but umbilical cord still intact towards end of delivery

Recognizing Problems

If labour does not progress or is prolonged, speedy action may be necessary to save the life of the mare and foal. Problems arise if the foal is:

❏ not being delivered in the right direction;

❏ if one of his legs is bent backwards (malpresentation, or dystocia); there is a tendency for this to happen in the foal because of his long limbs and neck. Dystocia can also be caused by problems with the dam, such as not straining properly. Sometimes, though this happens rarely, the dam's bony pelvis, through which the foal must be delivered, is too small.

There are three main reasons as to why equine dystocia is so serious:

❏ The mare will continue to push and strain even if the foal is stuck, until eventually her uterus ruptures, leading to peritonitis or fatal bleeding.

❏ During delivery the placenta separates quickly, and so the foal loses his oxygen supply and must breathe himself.

❏ The placenta is often retained following dystocia, with serious consequences if the mare is not treated.

The main clues that something is wrong include:

❏ If the glistening white amnion enclosing the front legs and the nose fails to appear within minutes after the waters have broken.

❏ If the red, velvet-like allantochorion appears at the vulval lips at the start of second stage, with no apparent fluid loss. This needs opening rapidly to allow safe passage of the foal and is commonly called a 'red bag' delivery.

❏ Repeated forceful straining but with nothing happening.

❏ No straining for lengthy periods once the amnion has appeared.

❏ The mare continually gets up and down and rolls from side to side.

❏ The foal is stuck at the hips once the head, legs and chest are out.

In all potential dystocia cases the vet should be contacted immediately a problem is identified. There is no time to spare, and it is better to call for help too soon rather than too late. It is sensible to alert your vet when the mare is due to foal. If the foal does not appear within 20 minutes of the mare lying down and straining hard, you need immediate veterinary help. In the rare case that a foal does become stuck, the vet may advise that the mare is kept up and walking round the box to reduce straining until help arrives.

An abnormal red bag delivery in a standing mare

Post-Foaling Problems

Unfortunately the hassles are not over once a mare has delivered her foal; indeed, the whole breeding process is fraught with potentially complicated and expensive emergencies including retained placenta, colic, mastitis and metritis.

Retained Placenta

This is a common complication, and describes the situation where the mare does not pass the afterbirth. Between 2 and 10 per cent of mares will fail to pass their placenta, or the whole of it, within three hours from foaling.

If the placenta is retained for more than three hours, contact a vet.

If nothing has happened after six hours, it should be considered as a potentially life-threatening emergency.

A retained placenta provides an open door for infection to enter the mare. If treated within hours, there are unlikely to be any long-term effects to either the mare or foal. Some mares will remain relatively well with a retained placenta, whilst others can die from it. It is a particularly dangerous condition in heavy horse breeds, where laminitis is a potentially serious complication. The rule is the bigger the horse, the more serious the problem, and the more urgently treatment should be initiated.

How you recognize this

If the placenta can be seen hanging from the back end of the mare, the problem is obvious. But the placenta may tear, and part may remain concealed internally. It is therefore a good idea to examine the membranes after delivery to ensure that nothing is missing. If you are unsure, ask a vet to check. The placenta is approximately 'Y' shaped, with the membranes attached to it, and there should be one obvious tear produced by the foal. Other tears are due to the mare standing on it, so piece it together like a jigsaw.

Occasionally the placenta is not visible, because

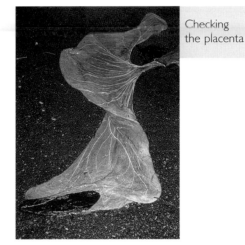

Checking the placenta

the foetal membranes have slipped forwards and remain inside the mare. An unusually dirty discharge may suggest this.

If a mare becomes ill within a couple of days of foaling, with a high temperature, loss of appetite, depression and laminitis, a retained placenta fragment should be suspected and a vet contacted immediately.

What you should do

- ❑ If there is any reason for concern – for instance, if the placenta is retained for more than three hours – you must contact a vet.
- ❑ If the membranes are dangling, it helps to tie a knot in them above the hocks. The feel of them against their legs alarms some mares, causing them to kick out, which could injure their foal.
- ❑ Do not tie a weight to the placenta in the hope of encouraging it to be expelled, as this may cause tearing and bleeding.

❑ A gentle tug and twist on the dangling placenta is worth attempting in case it has almost detached; however, no excessive force should be applied.

❑ Encourage the foal to suckle, as this stimulates the mare's body into producing hormones that cause the womb to contract and thereby shift the placenta.

❑ Gentle exercise, such as a five-minute walk, can also help.

What the vet can do

This depends on the individual case; however, the majority will respond to injections of oxytocin, which stimulates contractions to expel the placenta. This is also often given in the form of an intravenous drip. Occasionally the vet will need to distend the placenta with fluid to encourage it to come out. Antibiotic and anti-inflammatory drugs are also often prescribed, together with measures that will reduce the risk of laminitis.

Encourage the foal to suckle

Other Post-Foaling Emergencies

Most other post-foaling complications need urgent veterinary attention; these include uterine prolapse, colic, mastitis and metritis.

Uterine prolapse

On rare occasions the mare pushes out the whole womb or uterus following delivery of the foal. Fortunately this hardly ever happens, but if it does, call a vet at once. Immediate first aid whilst waiting involves restraining the mare and, if possible, covering the prolapse with a moistened sheet or towel to reduce further damage. It will also help reduce swelling if the prolapse can be held up at dock level. This will need plenty of help as it is heavy and requires two people, plus another two to steady the mare and foal.

Colic

Evidence of colic may indicate catastrophic internal bleeding, and should be taken seriously in a mare after foaling. There is the potential for the large bowel to displace into the gap left by the newborn, and if this happens, surgery may be needed.

Mastitis

The mare develops an infection of the udder.

Metritis

The mare develops a vaginal discharge, and shows signs of infection. This is usually associated with either a difficult delivery or the placenta being retained. Rapid aggressive veterinary treatment is needed to resolve this.

Management of Mare and Foal

The stress of foaling is more than compensated for by the arrival of a healthy foal. However, many problems can affect a growing foal, and these can have a profound effect on his future health. It is essential to watch them carefully, and treat them properly from the start.

Checklist for Mare and Foal

A foal is not a miniature version of an adult horse, but a newborn animal adapting to life in the big wide world. Both mare and foal should have a post-natal check by a vet, but there are important things for you to monitor as well.

- ❏ Does the foal seem to be breathing normally? Immediately after birth they gasp and breathe at a much faster rate than an adult horse.
- ❏ Is the foal bright, alert, and aware of his surroundings? A healthy foal will have a suck reflex within 20 minutes of birth. Usually they will try to stand within 30 minutes.

Normal heart and respiratory rates and rectal temperature of the foal

Age	Heart rate (beats/min)	Resp. rate (breaths/min)	Temp. 0°C (0°F)
1min	60–80	Gasping	37–39 (99–102)
15min	120–160	40–60	37–39 (99–102)
12hr	80–120	30–40	37–39 (99–102)
24hr	80–100	30	37–39 (99–102)

Checklist for Mare and Foal (continued)

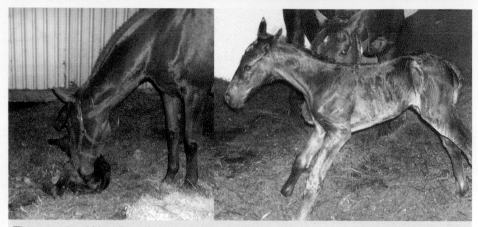

The mare should be allowed to bond with the foal; this she usually does by nuzzling. In response, the foal usually attempts to stand

❑ The foal should stand and suckle within 2 to 3 hours of birth. If a foal has shown no signs of trying to get up and feed within 3 to 4 hours, call a vet.

❑ The foal should pass his first droppings (known as 'meconium') within the first day of life. These are dark brown to black in colour, and can be very firm in consistency; paler milk dung will then follow.

❑ The foal should produce lots of dilute urine within 12 hours of birth.

❑ The gums of a foal should be a healthy pink colour; watch out for yellow gums, which are an indication of jaundice.

❑ The mare should welcome her foal without aggression. Occasionally a mare will reject the foal.

If the foal is to remain healthy, the mare must be well, too.

❑ Ensure that she is comfortable.

❑ After the foal has settled into a routine, any change from the normal pattern of behaviour, particularly sleeping more than usual, or going 'off suck' (failing to drink from their mother) should be taken seriously. Normal foals should suckle on average seven times an hour.

❑ Check the mare's udder to see if it is full. A distended udder is one of the first signs of a 'fading foal'.

❑ Either ensure that the foal is given anti-tetanus treatment soon after birth, or better still, ensure the dam is properly vaccinated in the last couple of months before foaling so that she can pass on the immunity to the foal.

❑ If you have any doubt about either foal or dam, discuss your concerns with a vet. Any foal abnormality or illness should be taken seriously. Do not rely on the first aid treatments you would try for an adult horse. In particular, you should contact a vet urgently if the foal:
• stops feeding;
• has diarrhoea;
• goes lame;
• has difficulty breathing.

The Importance of Colostrum

A newborn foal is born lacking a competent immune system, and to survive they must obtain antibodies (immunoglobulins) to protect them against disease. When the foal suckles the first milk (colostrum) from his dam he should receive these antibodies. In the first day of life the foal can absorb them through his gut to boost his own immunity.

Problems arise when a foal is too weak to suckle, because if he is then deprived of colostrum, this can push him on a downward spiral from which he will not recover. If a foal will not feed himself, it is vital either to bottle feed, or better still, arrange for your vet to stomach tube him with sufficient good quality colostrum.

Note that if the mare runs milk steadily before foaling, she can run out of colostrum for the foal. A vet can run tests to check the quality of the mare's colostrum, and how effective the foal's uptake has been. If there is a problem with colostrum uptake, which is technically known as 'failure of passive transfer', it is possible to boost the foal's immunity with a transfusion of plasma (the part of the blood that is rich in antibodies). This is given as an intra-venous drip, and can be lifesaving. If there is ever the opportunity, it is sensible to collect and freeze any spare colostrum – for instance, if a brood mare loses a foal – as it can help to save another life. Some studs and veterinary clinics try to maintain such a 'colostrum bank'.

Care of the navel

Care of the foal's umbilicus, or navel, is important to prevent the entry of infection. Always treat it with dilute antiseptic, such as chlorhexidine or pev-idine, two or three times a day after foaling. This is essential to reduce the risk of infection of the umbilicus itself ('navel ill') and serious infection elsewhere, particularly in the joints, when it would cause serious lameness known as 'joint ill' (see picture below).

Preventive Measures

- ❑ Keep the foaling box clean to reduce a build-up of infection.
- ❑ Clean up the mare, especially after foaling, and particularly around her hindquarters and udder, where the foal could pick up bugs as he hunts for the teat to start suckling. Breeders will have noticed the foal licking and nuzzling the mare as he looks for milk: if the mare is covered in manure and muck from foaling, it is likely that the unprotected foal will pick up infections.
- ❑ Disinfect the foal's navel.
- ❑ Ensure the foal ingests colostrum.
- ❑ Watch the foal and dam closely.
- ❑ Ensure early treatment to fight off infection.

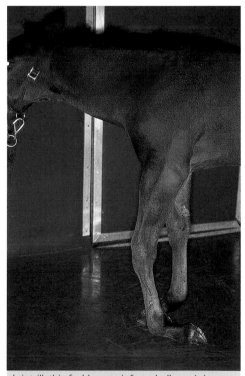

Joint ill: this foal has an infected elbow joint

Foal rolling with colic

The Management of Emergencies

Septicaemia (blood poisoning)

This is a term used to describe a bacterial infection that has spread to multiple organs via the bloodstream. It is a common cause of death in newborn foals less than one week old. Good management of both mare and foal is important in minimizing the likelihood of this disease. Insufficient colostrum increases the risk to the foal.

Meconium colics

This complication occurs in foals when the first droppings become impacted within the gut. The foal becomes constipated, usually in the first or second day of his life. In the early stages the foal may seem uncomfortable, and to be straining a lot.

First aid: To avoid this straining, many people routinely administer an enema to newborn foals. This usually resolves the problem, but occasionally there is a serious blockage with severe colic. More drastic veterinary attention may then be needed, such as liquid paraffin by stomach tube, intravenous fluids, painkillers, and rarely surgery.

Bladder rupture

This is a more common problem in colts than in fillies, but on the whole it is less common than meconium retention, with which it is often confused. The way to tell these apart is that foals that are straining to pass droppings arch their back, whilst those straining to urinate sink their back. A foal with a ruptured bladder will only pass tiny dribbles of urine frequently. They are normal at birth but deteriorate when a few days old as the urine accumulating internally makes them ill. Watch for a large belly, which is literally filling up with the urine leaking from the bladder, and contact a vet as soon as you notice a problem. Treatment involves stabilizing the urine-poisoned systems, and then surgery to repair the bladder.

Foal rejection

Occasionally a mare – and in particular if they have not had a foal before – will reject their foal, or not allow him to suckle. It will help if the mare's udder is handled during pregnancy, so she is accustomed to something touching her teats in advance of the foal's arrival. When a mare rejects her foal, the following measures will help:

❏ Try feeding the mare concentrates to distract her while the foal suckles.
❏ Check for medical conditions that cause a painful udder. Consult a vet for this.
❏ The vet may administer a sedative or tranquillizer to calm the mare. Avoid any painful restraint, as this will only stress her more.

❏ A desperate and potentially dangerous measure is to turn the mare and foal out with other horses in an attempt to encourage maternal behaviour in the mare. If you do take this course of action, however, you need to observe closely all the time.
❏ Sometimes you may end up milking the mare and feeding the foal his colostrum by bottle or stomach tube.

The Orphan Foal

A foal may be orphaned by the following circumstances:

❏ death of the mare;
❏ rejection by the mare;
❏ illness of the mare;
❏ disease of the foal;
❏ management reasons.

Orphans are difficult to rear, and frequently develop behavioural problems later in life. In the long term it therefore helps to foster a foal, rather than to hand rear it.

Foals can usually be trained to feed from a bucket or bowl from a young age. However, it is important to avoid the foal becoming spoilt and 'humanized', so some form of equine company – maybe an old pony – is vitally important if the foal is to develop normal equine behaviour patterns.

During the first 2 days a healthy 50kg foal will consume 5–7ltr of mare's milk, and should be fed every 1–2 hours. The foal's intake will increase rapidly over the next week, rising to 12–15ltr per day, then steadily increasing at about 23–28% bodyweight per day. A good quality milk replacer should be used. Calf and lamb milk replacers are not suitable. In the UK, there is a National Foaling Bank (telephone: 01952 811234, fax number 01952 811202) which can provide vital advice and assistance in these circumstances. It is sensible to join the National Foaling Bank, as you never know when you may need their help.

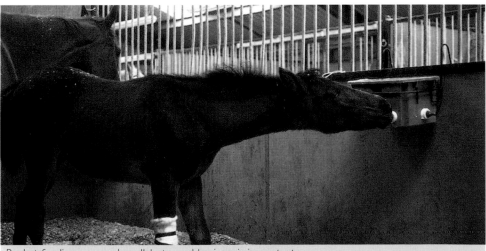
Bucket feeding can work well, but good hygiene is important

Stallion Emergencies

A stallion can sustain kick injuries when attempting to cover an uncooperative mare, or if he is attacked by another horse. There is a risk of trauma to the penis and testicles, and early treatment is important to prevent future complications that could limit their reproductive performance. It is therefore essential to contact a vet straightaway.

First aid action

❑ Cold hosing or cooling with ice packs will help to control swelling.

❑ Apply pressure or a bandage to control bleeding and swelling.

❑ Support the penis using cotton sheet or similar to prevent further damage. Essentially this means rigging up a truss to support the area of damage; a pair of tights works well.

❑ Your vet will administer painkillers and anti-inflammatories. Occasionally with injuries to the penis, bleeding may be profuse and surgery may be required.

Truss for penile prolapse

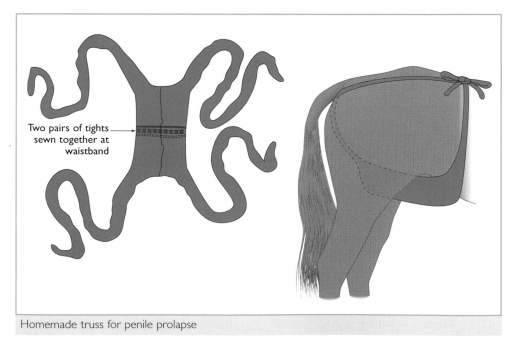

Two pairs of tights sewn together at waistband

Homemade truss for penile prolapse

A Protruding Penis

The inability of a stallion or gelding to retract his penis inside the sheath is an emergency. It can occur for several reasons, including general debilitation, or occasionally following sedation; it is normal for the penis to drop for up to an hour following sedation. Stallions are said to be more susceptible to this complication following sedation with ACP than geldings. As regards first aid, the following course of action is advised:

❑ Establish and remove the cause where possible.
❑ Clean the area with mild cleansers and antiseptic cream or petroleum jelly.
❑ Attempt to reduce any swelling, and support the prolapsed penis with some form of truss.
❑ Bring the horse in, particularly if it is below freezing point, to avoid additional damage.
❑ Contact your vet if the condition persists for more than an hour.

Colic in a Stallion

A twisted testicle or scrotal hernia are two possible serious causes of colic in a stallion, both of which conditions will require surgery. It is essential to contact a vet immediately if your stallion has colic with an unusual swelling in the genital area. Failure to act can result in infertility and other major problems.

Castration Complications

Castration is the most common equine surgery, yet the risks should be considered and the approach selected that will best minimize these. In mature horses (more than 3 years) the procedure may be best performed under general anaesthesia.

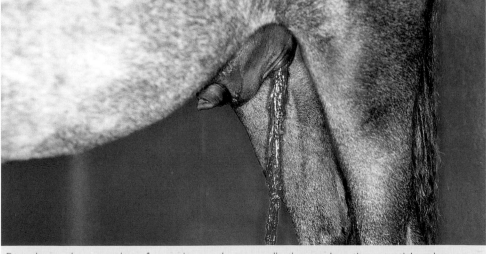

Even the routine operation of castration can have complications, such as the potential prolapse of tissue from the surgical site as shown here. Other complications include bleeding or infection

Euthanasia

The humane destruction of any horse is an emotive issue, but almost every horse owner will probably be involved with it at some stage. A decision on euthanasia (defined as 'a good death') can be stressful, especially if it has to be made quickly, and all the more so if subsequently you feel it was made in haste, and is one you regret. It is therefore worth considering the whole serious issue in advance so that you know what you want for your horse. And if others know your intentions, they can make any such decision in your absence, should something serious happen to your horse when you cannot be contacted. As a vet, I have more than once been faced with a situation where a horse has to be put down and the owner is either unconscious and on their way to hospital as part of the same emergency, or is away on holiday. So please leave instructions!

Amongst the questions that need to be answered are insurance, and the method of destruction.

Is the Horse Insured?
First, do the insurers need to be notified before you can proceed? In general the best advice is to contact the insurers before anything irreversible is done. In a crisis where the horse is badly injured – for instance, if he has an untreatable broken leg – then it is justified to put the horse down immediately in order to prevent their further suffering. The key word here is 'untreatable', since many conditions can be

However much you might want to ignore the possibility of euthanasia, the whole event can be made less traumatic if you have planned how you want it to be dealt with

treated, even though this may not at first seem to be an option. An example is a horse with severe colic pain, when it might be thought that immediate euthanasia were justified; in fact the colic might be curable by surgery. If you proceed without seeking the insurer's permission you may later be unable to make a claim. Your vet will be able to advise you.

It is also important to find out if the insurers need a second opinion from another vet before your horse is put down, and/or if they require a post mortem afterwards. It helps to clarify this, as it may resolve other issues, such as where and how euthanasia is performed

Where should Euthanasia be Performed?

This is very much up to the individual. Most vets and knackermen will come to your own yard, so the horse can be put to sleep in familiar surroundings. But some owners will prefer the horse to be taken elsewhere, such as either to the vet's or the

Methods of Euthanasia

Traditionally with horses euthanasia was performed by shooting using a free bullet.

Advantages
❑ When performed correctly, death is very rapid.
❑ The carcass can be disposed of easily.
❑ It is cheap.

Disadvantages
❑ It is aesthetically unpleasant to some people.
❑ It is potentially dangerous, so may not be practical, for instance if it has to be carried out in a public place.
❑ Both a knowledge of firearms and a license are required, and not all vets or knackermen have the training or license for this. Some knackermen will expect the euthanasia to be performed by the vet, and sometimes vice versa. Frequently the vet will sedate the horse for the knackerman.

Methods of euthanasia
Alternatively euthanasia may be performed using intravenous lethal agents, which many people find less distressing. Prior placement of an intravenous catheter facilitates the procedure, although it can be traumatic in a needle-shy horse. There are, however, ways around this, such as giving sedatives in the feed in advance. The whole intention is to make the procedure as stress free as possible, although inevitably there are situations when this can be extremely difficult.

Carcass disposal
Disposal of the carcass must be carefully considered, particularly following lethal injection; the options are usually cremation/incineration, or burial with appropriate permission. Note that in 2003, regulations changed in the UK preventing the burial of farm animals; however, it is still possible to bury pets. In fact it is not clear where horses fit in, and it may be best to contact direct the Department for Environment Food and Rural Affairs (DEFRA, see www.defra.gov.uk), who currently (April 2004) advise discussing individual circumstances with the local authority (usually the trading standards department).

The UK's Sidmouth Donkey Sanctuary has recommended that if one of a pair of donkeys is destroyed, the other is left with it for some hours

knackerman's premises, and this may be more practical if a post mortem is required. Removal of the carcass can be distressing for observers and difficult in a muddy field, so this may be a reason for moving the horse elsewhere first. Another option is to go to a licensed slaughterhouse, or to ask the hunt kennelman to come, if he is available.

Does the owner need to be there?

Again, whether you are present is very much up to the individual. This situation can be extremely difficult for the owner, who is probably better remembering the horse in happier times; it is rarely essential for them to be there. Informed consent, often in writing, may be needed from the owners, especially if they are not present.

What about other horses?

If there are several horses in a field and one is seriously injured and must be put down, what should be done with the others?

Frequently if the other horses are taken away the injured horse becomes distressed, which is the last thing one wants: the welfare of the injured horse should always take priority. In fact the others are rarely disturbed for more than a moment as they will not comprehend what is happening; furthermore it is said to help the others settle if they see the body. Certainly the Donkey Sanctuary has recommended that if one of a pair of donkeys is destroyed, the other should be left with it for some hours. The same applies to a mare – leaving the dead foal in the box for a time will help the mare settle.

Further Information

Further information about euthanasia and the related issues can be found in the booklet *Farewell: Making the Right Decision*, published by the Humane Slaughter Association, The Old School House, Brewhouse Hill, Wheathampstead, Herts AL4 8AN; email: info@hsa.org.uk; tel 01582 831919.

Insurance

A horse is an expensive purchase, hence insurance should always be considered. Furthermore, not only is there a need to cover the costs of illness, injury or theft of a horse, but horse ownership also brings with it the risk of an accident involving serious injury to yourself, or legal liability for an accident. In an emergency it is essential to know exactly what insurance cover you have for your horse, and unfortunately we are all guilty of not reading the small print until problems arise: most disputed insurance claims concerning horses are due to basic misunderstandings as to the level of insurance cover purchased initially.

Understanding Insurance Cover

All risks mortality (ARM) This is basically 'death' or mortality insurance, which is designed to pay a claim if a horse dies or is destroyed as a result of an incurable illness or injury. In fact this cover is very limited, and only covers terminal conditions such as irreparable fractures. It does not cover conditions where the horse can potter around a paddock, but can no longer perform the work that is expected of them. This can be a big source of dispute. An example is the point-to-pointer that has sustained a serious tendon injury, so it is decided to have the horse destroyed because he can no longer race. When an insurance claim under an ARM policy is submitted, the insured is dismayed when it

is turned down. Such a horse would potentially be paddock sound given time and appropriate care, so does not count as a mortality claim. Vets and insurers have strict guidelines, which have to be fulfilled for this sort of insurance to pay out. In summary, it has to be a condition that the horse is going to die from, and could not recover, despite treatment. Such situations are few and far between, especially with modern veterinary technology. In the US, this is humane destruction cover and such claims are clearly based on medical, not economic grounds.

Permanent loss of use (PLU) This insurance cover is designed to pay out if a horse is permanently incapacitated so that he cannot carry out the function for which he is insured. This is a far more comprehensive cover and accordingly has a much higher premium. There can be difficulty in confirming that a horse is

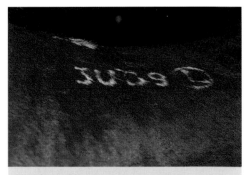

A circled L freeze brand means the horse has been the subject of a loss of use insurance claim

indeed totally unable to work forever as insured. If a horse is kept in retirement following a loss of use claim, it will usually be freeze branded with an L for 'loss of use' in order to distinguish his status.

Veterinary fees insurance This is designed to cover the costs of veterinary treatment. There will be a limit on how much an insurance will cover for any one condition, and it is important to establish what this is, as well as how long the cover will remain in force. Veterinary fees are a common reason for claims so will substantially increase the cost of your

policy. Most insurance companies will ask you to pay a certain amount of each claim (known as the excess).

Personal liability insurance This is vital for horses and is known as 'Third party cover' in the UK. It can be obtained by membership of many equine organizations such as the British Horse Society (as a gold member), the Pony Club, and various other equine organizations. As a horse owner, you could be legally liable for any damage your horse caused; for instance, if he strayed on to the public highway and was the cause of a traffic accident.

A horse being positioned for surgey under general anaesthesia. Equine surgery is potentially a costly procedure involving much manpower and sophisticated equipment

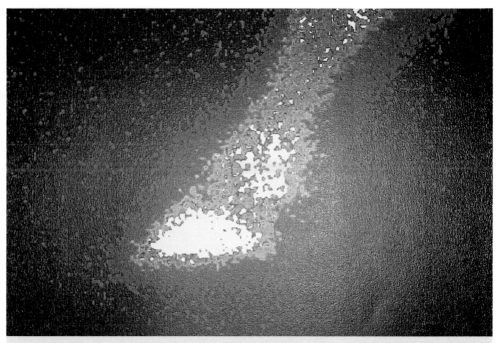

An example of a bone scan image of a horse's foot, which is a costly (£500 plus) procedure used to pinpoint lameness and investigate other problems

Other insurance cover This may include personal accident and possibly dental cover. Many insurance companies will provide benefits for permanent disability or death to protect anyone handling or riding your horse. Other options include cover for theft of the horse or any equipment.

Understanding the Complications

Exclusions Remember that almost all equine insurance in the UK is offered as an annual contract with a time limit. This varies with different policies, so that you can only claim for a limited period. After a year the policy is reviewed. If there has been a claim, it is likely that an exclusion will be applied when you come to renew

your policy, so preventing you claiming for the same or a similar problem in future. Most companies will review certain exclusions after a period of time without recurrence of the particular problem.

Pre-existing conditions If a condition was present before the insurance policy was taken out, insurers are unlikely to consider it their responsibility if it flares up at a later date. Insurers will carefully investigate the horse's history before settling any claim, so it is important to declare all facts at the start.

Failure to inform insurers Always notify your insurers about all possible claims as soon as possible. Try to contact them, ideally in advance, to obtain their permission to proceed with any surgery, major treatment, or with having your horse put down. In the sad situation that your horse dies, you must confirm with your insurers whether a post mortem is required. If they are going to pay out, they are entitled to know all the facts.

Insurance varies from country to country

What applies in one country may be quite different in another. For this reason, it is recommended you seek professional help to understand insurance implications in your country as well deciphering the small print.

Key Points for an Emergency

Know what insurance cover you have, so that in an emergency you can make sensible and realistic decisions. For example, there is no point agreeing to submit your horse to costly colic surgery, which you cannot afford personally, if your insurance already has an exclusion in place as a result of previous episodes of colic.

Have copies of all insurance documentation available, so that vet and owner can confirm their insurance status immediately the horse is injured or unwell.

Tell your insurance company what is happening to your horse. Many have out-of-hours helplines for this purpose.

2 Coping with General Emergencies

In this section

Making Emergency Calls

In a serious emergency it may be necessary to telephone for professional help. In the UK the traditional number to ring, and the one that has been in use since 1937, is 999 – although the EU number 112 is just as valid. The emergency services that can be contacted via either of these numbers are:

❑ police;

❑ fire service;

❑ ambulance;

❑ coastguard;

❑ mountain rescue;

❑ cave rescue.

The last two services are contacted via the police. In the US the emergency number is 911. Emergency calls are free and can be made from any phone, including most mobile and car phones. On motorways in the UK, emergency telephones can be found every mile, with marker posts between them indicating the direction of the one closest to you. These phones simply need to be picked up to be answered.

Always carry the telephone number of your vet on you when riding out, as some emergencies may require veterinary attention but do not merit a 999 call. Don't rely on the number being in the address feature of your mobile phone in case for some reason you are unable to access the information.

Mobile Phones

A mobile phone is a piece of technology that is definitely worth investing in, and has proved to be a life-saving piece of equipment on some occasions. Even if you are only walking up to a nearby field to visit your horse, don't forget to take it with you; if there is a problem you can save valuable time by being able to ring for help immediately, rather than having to rush back to the yard to raise the alarm. You will also then be able to remain on the scene whilst waiting for aid to arrive.

Be sure to observe the following code of conduct with your phone:

❑ Make sure you keep the battery charged up.

❑ Switch the phone off or to silent/vibrate during normal riding or handling activities with your horse, in case someone rings and the noise alarms him. Similarly, don't try and use the phone at such times to chat to friends either, because it will distract your attention and you will not be fully in control.

❑ If you need to make an emergency call from a mobile phone, remember to tell the operator the county and district you are in, as mobile network operators may be based a considerable distance away from you, and won't know your location. When you have finished your call, be sure to leave it switched on so that the emergency services can call you back if necessary.

❑ Unfortunately mobile phones are not foolproof, and have their limitations; thus in some places, particularly more hilly or remote areas, the signal may be weak or even non-existent. When riding out it is therefore a good idea to carry both a phone card and change as 'back-up' to your mobile, just in case you need to use a public payphone instead.

What To Say

❑ On dialling 999, the operator will ask you which service(s) you need, and will put you through to the appropriate control officer. Should human casualties be involved, ask for the ambulance service; if necessary the control officer can pass on messages to other emergency services.

❑ At this point you may be feeling anxious and frightened, and consequently inclined to gabble; take a deep breath to help clear your thoughts, and calm yourself so that you can speak slowly and clearly, and can give accurate and concise information. You should state the following:

• Your name.

• The telephone number you are ringing from.

• The exact location of the accident, including road names, numbers, junctions and any landmarks. If you are calling from a payphone your location will be displayed inside it.

• The type of accident and how serious it is.

• The number, sex and approximate age of any casualties, plus any other known details about the nature of their injuries.

• Any other relevant information; for example, any hazards such as power-line damage, or weather or ground conditions such as snow, ice, or boggy terrain that may cause difficulties for rescue vehicles.

❑ Do not hang up until the control officer has cleared the line.

❑ If you have to leave a casualty alone in order to fetch help, take any vital first aid action first (see Part 3: First Aid for People), make your call brief but accurate, and then return as quickly as possible. If you send someone else for help, ask them to report back to you after calling for help.

Everyday Emergency Kit

You never know where or when an emergency will occur, so you should always carry with you:

❑ a mobile phone

❑ a pocket knife: the sturdy, folding survival type with a variety of tools is useful, and can be kept in a pouch attached to your belt.

At the yard, the following items should always be kept in an easily accessible place:

❑ first aid kit (human and equine);

❑ current list of emergency phone numbers;

❑ tools for simple maintenance jobs;

❑ shoeing kit;

❑ wire cutters.

Restraining Horses

When handling any horse, whether it is during the course of routine care or for examination or treatment, some form of restraint will be required. At its most basic this may be no more than a headcollar and leadrope, but with an animal that is maybe frightened and/or in pain this may not be sufficient to ensure efficient treatment and the safety of both horse and handler, and you may need to use a bridle or even a Chifney (anti-rearing bit). It may also on occasion be necessary to use other forms of restraint in order to facilitate certain rescue operations, administer treatment, or control the horse in a situation he perhaps finds frightening: this might be by means of holding up a foreleg, with a twitch, or by sedating the horse.

Using a Headcollar

A headcollar should be the correct size and fit, preferably with room for further adjustment if required; you can tie a knot in the end of the leadrope for additional grip. Remember the following code of practice:

❑ Do not slip your fingers through the headcollar noseband, as they may become trapped.
❑ Do not wrap the leadrope around your hand for better grip; if the horse pulls away from you the rope may tighten and crush your hands.
❑ Wear gloves to protect the hands from burns and provide better grip.
❑ Another way of increasing restraint is to take a fold of loose skin on the neck just in front of the shoulders, hold it tightly in a closed fist, and twist it slightly.

A headcollar and leadrope may be sufficient in minor incidents

Using a Bridle

A bridle can give more control than a headcollar if you remember the following:
❑ Ensure that both noseband (if present) and throatlash are buckled up.
❑ If a martingale is attached, remove it.
❑ Take both reins over the horse's head.
❑ If there are no reins on the bridle, pass a lead-rope through one bit ring, beneath the lower jaw and clip it onto the opposite bit ring.
❑ For firmer control, a Chifney (anti-rearing bit) can be useful. This is usually attached to a sliphead, and a leadrope clipped to the ring on the lower part of the bit.

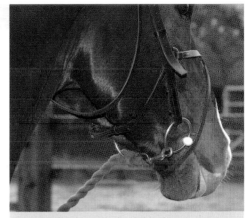

Attach a leadrope to both bit rings to prevent it being pulled through the mouth

Lifting a Foreleg

If the horse is inclined to fidget or is likely to kick out with a back foot, holding up a forefoot may help. You will need one person to hold the head and another to hold the foot, and should always remember the following:
❑ Always hold up a front foot, never a back one.
❑ If a foreleg is being treated, hold up the opposite forefoot.
❑ If a back leg is being treated, hold up the forefoot on the same side (but not if the back leg has to be held up).
❑ If an area of the body is being treated, hold up a forefoot on the same side as the other person is working.
❑ Do not attempt to pick up a forefoot if another limb is already being held up by someone else.
❑ Gloves should be worn in order to protect the hands from damage should the horse start snatching its foot away.
❑ How you hold the foot up is also important: you should hold the wall of the hoof near the toe, and keep the elbow, knee and fetlock joints flexed just enough that the foot cannot easily be pulled away. Do not flex them so much that it causes discomfort (particularly with arthritic

Hold the leg from the side: do not stand in front. Although it appears as though the horse is under complete control, our handlers should be wearing hard hats for their safety

horses), or hold the foot so high that it leads to loss of balance. Also, some horses may find it tiring if asked to stand on three legs for any length of time, and may then fight to try and put the fourth down again.
❑ Holding up a forefoot is not by any means fool-proof, and you should be aware that some horses may rear, plunge forwards or struggle violently to free themselves. Neither will it entirely prevent a determined horse from kicking out with a back foot – and though it may not be delivered with full force, such blows can still be severe.

Using a Twitch

Pressure applied to the horse's top lip can have a calming effect; this is known as the 'endorphin reaction'. Either the fingertips can be used to firmly grasp the top lip (although this is tiring and also requires a certain degree of finger strength to be effective), or a twitch can be used, either a rope twitch or a 'humane' twitch.

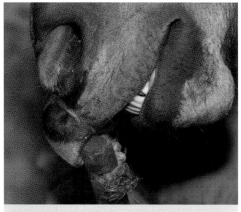

Using a rope twitch. Ideally the baler twine would be replaced with a smoother cord

Rope twitch

Place one wrist through the rope loop, grasp the horse's top lip firmly with the fingertips, and then slip the rope up over your hand and tighten it by twisting the wooden handle.

'Humane' twitch

Put one hand between the two shaped rigid bars, and take a firm hold of the top lip with the fingers. Use the other hand to slide the twitch up onto the lip with the hinged part pointing upwards, and close the two rigid sides firmly onto it. The tension is maintained by wrapping the drawstring around the lower ends of the two bars and securing it.

Watchpoints

❏ Check that the edges of the lips are curled inwards, so they are less likely to be cut. If the horse throws its head about, allow the hand

holding the twitch to go with the movement, otherwise it is likely to be pulled off.

❏ Allow a few minutes for the twitch to take effect; the head may droop a little, and the eyes develop a slightly glazed, introspective appearance.

❏ A twitch can be highly effective on some horses, but less so on others; if the horse becomes agitated, take the twitch off straightaway. A twitch should not be used for more than 15 minutes.

❏ Take care when taking off a twitch, as the horse may throw his head around as he is being loosened but before it is fully removed, and there is a danger that it could hit the handler in the face. Rub the top lip briskly to help restore circulation to the area.

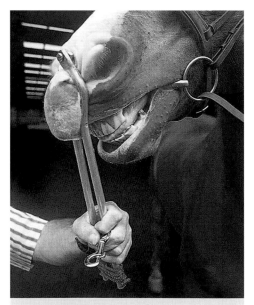

Using a 'humane' twitch

Using a Twitch

A twitch is too painful to use for more than fifteen minutes, and often tends to have reduced effect after this length of time anyway.

Sedating a Horse

In some instances sedation, or even anaesthesia, may offer the safest way to keep a horse under control; though do not administer any oral sedatives yourself whilst waiting for the vet to arrive. Sedation may seem an expensive option, but in fact it is frequently kinder and better for the horse, and safer for all concerned.

❑ If sedation is required, the vet will usually administer an intravenous injection, which is faster acting and has a more reliable depth of effect than other methods.

❑ As the sedative takes effect, the head will droop and the eyes appear glazed; the lips also become slack and the eyelids half close. In geldings and colts, the penis may be dropped.

❑ Some horses seem more susceptible to the effects of sedation than others; it is therefore important to keep a watchful eye on the horse the whole time it is under sedation in case he begins to pull out of it more rapidly than anticipated.

Following sedation

❑ Avoid moving the horse more than necessary until he has recovered from the effects, as balance and co-ordination will be affected.

❑ Do not feed until the sedation has worn off.

❑ Monitor the horse during recovery, especially if he is in a stable, when you should check him regularly in case he becomes cast due to disorientation and lack of spatial awareness.

❑ If the horse is turned out, place him in a small paddock with level ground, safe fencing, and on its own so that other horses won't hassle him.

❑ If it is absolutely necessary to transport the horse from the scene of an emergency whilst under the effects of sedation, an equine ambulance equipped with a sling may be used. Unfortunately ambulances are not often available, in which case it will be necessary to wait until the sedation has worn off sufficiently so that the horse is fit to travel safely; ask your vet.

Restraining a Fallen Horse

Sometimes when a horse is down it may be necessary to stop him trying to get up in order to prevent further injury – for instance, if he is cast and you are having to wait for help. This can be done by kneeling or sitting on its neck just behind the head, preferably from the spine side rather than the throat side: in this way pressure is not placed on the windpipe, and you are also out of the way of the front feet; if the horse cannot raise its head he will be unable to get up. Covering the eyes at the same time may also help to discourage any efforts to stand up.

It is better to restrain a fallen horse from the spine side, not the throat side

Safety for the Handler

The safety of the handler is paramount. Make sure someone is positioned at the horse's head. Although your vet may be used to working without a hard hat, you should not

Anyone helping to hold an injured horse should observe the following practices:

❑ Hold the horse in preference to tying him up.

❑ Always wear a hard hat, gloves and sturdy footwear, even if the horse is normally placid.

❑ Never stand directly in front of the horse, but to the side where you will have more control, and will not get knocked over or injured if he suddenly lunges forwards or rears.

❑ Whenever possible, stand on the same side as the person treating or examining the horse, unless this is impractical or you are specifically directed otherwise.

❑ Raising your voice, shouting or hitting the horse is likely to make him more fractious; try to remain calm, and use a soothing tone.

❑ Remember that maintaining a constant heavy and restrictive tension on the head may make some horses feel trapped and panicky, causing them to pull back or rear.

❑ Do not jerk roughly or abruptly at the horse's head, as this could well cause him to react by throwing his head up, pulling back

or rearing, and it only increases the 'fear' factor.

❑ In cold weather, throw a rug or a jacket over a clipped horse: feeling chilly may cause him to fidget more.

❑ Concentrate on what you are doing.

Examining the Horse Indoors and Out

If you are outside, first secure the area as well as you can – shut all yard gates or other potential routes of escape – and second, if possible, select the most level, least slippery piece of ground. If the horse is to be examined or treated indoors, be sure of the following safety factors:

❑ The lighting must be adequate.

❑ Enough bedding must be put down to ensure reasonably non-slip footing.

❑ Water and feed buckets should be taken out of the stable.

❑ Any droppings should be removed, as they can prove slippery underfoot if trodden in.

❑ The bottom door should be closed to prevent the horse from attempting to barge out.

Horse Rears when Led

Always make sure the equipment you use for leading will give you adequate control (see Restraining Horses, page 104).

A horse being led may rear as a response to pressure from the halter

❑ Wear a hard hat, gloves and sensible footwear when leading any horse, not just those individuals you know or suspect may be difficult.

❑ Be sure that the leadrope or leadrein used is long enough for you to move out of harm's way if the horse does rear.

❑ If you are using a headcollar to lead, clip the leadrope to the ring on the side of the noseband, rather than the one directly beneath the horse's lower jaw. This reduces poll pressure, which may cause a sensitive horse to rear; it is also less likely to become entangled in his front feet should he go up.

❑ If the horse does rear, slacken the pressure on the leadrope – do not pull on it, as this may make him go up even higher, and he then may lose his balance and fall over.

❑ Do not stand in front of him, but move to the side so you are out of the way of his front legs.

Horse Pulls Away whilst being Led

Use equipment that will give you sufficient control when leading a horse that is inclined to pull forwards or sideways away from the handler (see Restraining Horses, page 104).

Refer to Horse Rears when Led, above, for equipment and method of leading.

❑ If he starts to get ahead of you, keep his head and neck flexed towards your own body and turn him in a circle around you. If his shoulders pass you, and it is clear that you no longer have control but are being towed after him, there is a good chance that you will be dragged after him – or possibly be on the receiving end of a kick from a back foot as he draws even further ahead. If you reach this point of no return, let go of the leadrope rather than risk injury.

❑ If the horse persists in behaving like this, it would be as well to lead him in a bridle (see Restraining Horses, page 104).

Turning your horse in a circle around you will stop him marching on ahead of you

Fire and Theft

Fire see also Fire Prevention p166

Notices detailing the action to be taken in the event of a fire should be displayed in prominent locations around the yard, and all staff and horse owners should take the time to make themselves familiar with the information. It is also a good idea to hold regular fire drills.

Stable yards and ancillary buildings are often constructed from, and contain, highly inflammable materials, so if fire gets a hold it can often sweep rapidly through them with devastating effects. It is therefore essential that prompt action is taken on discovering a fire.

On finding a fire

❑ **Raise the alarm immediately – sound the fire bell.**

❑ **Ring for the emergency fire service (see Making Emergency Calls, page 102).**

❑ **Evacuate people and horses.**

❑ **Only attempt to tackle the fire if it is safe to do so.**

Evacuation of Premises

On hearing the alarm, all those not involved in equine evacuation should follow this procedure:

❑ Leave the premises immediately, shutting doors, and without stopping to collect up belongings.

❑ Do not attempt to re-enter any of the buildings, but go directly to the assembly point specified on the fire notice.

❑ Designate one responsible person to check that all the buildings are empty, and others to evacuate horses.

❑ Release the horses into a suitable, securely fenced paddock, preferably one where direct access from the yard is available; its location should also be displayed on the fire notice.

❑ If it is safe to do so, and headcollars and lead-ropes are ready to hand, the horses may be led out to the field. Some horses may become fearful at the sight and sound of fire and the smell of smoke, and refuse to leave their stables; covering the eyes with a damp cloth or jacket, making sure that the nostrils are not covered, may help.

❑ If the threat of fire is more urgent, do not waste time trying to lead horses out individually, but simply open the access gates through to the paddock, and then open all the stable doors and herd the horses out in a group. At all times be careful of personal safety when dealing with horses, which may be in a state of extreme fear or panic. Once the stables are empty, shut both top and bottom doors, provided it is still safe to approach the buildings to do so.

See also

❑ **Caught up in a Headcollar, page 127**
❑ **Horse Rears When Being Led, page 109**
❑ **Horse Pulls Away When Being Led, page 109**

Theft see also Security p164

Having a horse stolen is a devastating and traumatic event for an owner. In such a situation it is most important to take action as promptly as possible – with every moment you waste, your horse could be further away from you.

❑ First check quickly to ensure that the horse has not in fact been brought into a stable, or moved to a different field by someone else. If the horse is kept out at grass, check the fencing to see if it is a case of escape rather than theft (see Straying, page 123).

❑ If it does appear that the horse has been stolen, ring the police immediately. Try not to disturb things more than possible until they arrive. Be prepared to be both insistent and persistent about action being taken, since although this is an emergency for you, unless the crime is actually taking place it will be less of a priority to them.

❑ If the horse is marked in some way, contact the company it is registered with.

❑ In cases where a marked horse has been stolen, there is a chance that it will be abandoned once the thieves realize this, so ring local vets too in case they are called to attend to an injured horse that has been found wandering loose.

❑ Notify your local Horsewatch group; if you do not know who this is, contact your local riding club or an equine welfare organization who may be able to tell you, or look for details on the Internet.

❑ Contact newspapers and local radio stations: place advertisements in equine magazines and at livery yards, riding centres and at saddlery shops, feed merchants and other equine retail outlets.

❑ Find out the dates of sales being held within a 250-mile radius – many thefts take place just before auctions. Notify ports and slaughterhouses within this radius too, and also ask the police dealing with your case to notify their opposite numbers in these areas.

❑ Check your insurance policy to see if cover for theft is included: notify the company and find out if help with rewards is offered as a part of the cover.

❑ Try to attend auctions personally wherever possible, as some sales go on outside the sale ring – remember to take ID of the horse for proof. Look closely at all horses that are of a similar size, age, colour and sex – remember that distinctive markings can be concealed, and trimming can also change the horse's appearance to some extent.

❑ There are also horse-tracing websites on the Internet that you can look up; many of these will allow you to post your details free of charge.

Escaping from the Stable

Some horses are expert at sliding open the top bolt on the bottom door of their stable. If this is the case, fit an enclosed, horse-proof bolt; do not use a leadrope clip, as many horses learn how to unfasten them, and they also risk injuring their lip.

What To Do

❏ If a horse manages to escape from his stable or becomes loose on the yard, **before you do anything else, close all of the exits from the yard**.

❏ Be careful when you approach the horse to recapture him, as some may not want to be caught, and will turn and kick out. Use food to engage his interest and co-operation.

❏ Slip a rope around his neck just behind the ears before you attempt to put the headcollar on.

Barging out of the Stable

When entering a horse's stable, take care that he does not attempt to barge past you.

What To Do

❏ Always undo the lower bolt of the bottom door first, so that you can control both the movement of the door and of the horse whilst entering the stable.

❏ Open the door only as much as necessary to permit your entry, closing and bolting it securely behind you until you have caught the horse.

❏ Do not leave doors ajar whilst mucking out or handling the horse, unless he has been tied up.

❏ As you enter, place a hand on the horse's chest to push him back away from the doorway. If he continues to push determinedly past you and you cannot stop him, move quickly out of the way so he does not knock you over or crush you against the door frame as he goes past (see Escaping from the Stable, above).

❏ Fit a webbing gate or a slip rail at chest height across the inside of the doorway to prevent the horse barging out like this.

Webbing gate

Aggressive Horses see also Bullying p122

Aggressive behaviour is often incorrectly interpreted, and may in fact be a defensive response made when the horse feels he has no other option available to him. However, some genuinely nasty characters do exist, where there is no real explanation for such behaviour. Certain circumstances will make horses react competitively– for example, if you go into a yard or a field of horses carrying a bucket of feed – and aggressive behaviour will then almost certainly erupt amongst the group as they vie for the food.

What To Do

❑ If you are attempting to catch a horse in the stable or yard, and he presents his quarters to you, do not risk getting kicked. Instead, encourage him to bring his head round to face you, so you can put on the headcollar safely; offer the bribe of a little food from your hand if necessary.

❑ If the horse is out in the yard or field with others, it is best to bring in those other ones first before going to catch the difficult individual, so as to avoid fights breaking out amongst them.

❑ If a horse lunges at you with his teeth, get yourself out of the way as fast as possible.

❑ If you are stranded at the back of the stable or yard, or in the middle of a field, you will not be able to get past the horse or to outrun him, so use whatever you have to hand to make yourself appear bigger and make the horse back off – swing a headcollar or bridle round, and wave your arms and shout loudly; like this you can then slowly work your way back towards the stable door or the field gate.

❑ If you have been engaged in a chore such as mucking out or picking up droppings, you can use your wheelbarrow to form a barrier between you.

❑ If a horse suddenly begins to display aggressive behaviour that is out of character, examine every aspect of his management and ask your vet to check him over.

Try to appear bigger to make an aggressive horse back off

Coping with a Cast Horse

The term 'cast' is used to describe a horse lying on his side and unable to rise because his legs are too close to the stable wall or fence, or the camber of the ground is such that he cannot get his legs underneath his body in order to get up. This usually happens because the horse has either rolled right over, or lain down too close to a wall, fence or bank. Many horses panic and struggle violently which can lead to injuries and exhaustion. If he remains cast for any length of time, breathing difficulties may occur due to the bulk of his body compressing the lung on the side in contact with the ground.

What To Do

❑ Seek assistance immediately; two lunge lines and two strong assistants will be needed. All those assisting should wear hard hats, gloves and sensible footwear.

❑ Keep the horse as still and quiet as possible whilst waiting for help, and also while any lunge reins are being attached, by having one person sit or kneel on the neck just behind the cheekbone (see Restraining a Fallen Horse, page 107).

❑ If the horse is wearing an anti-cast roller, remove it, if necessary by cutting through the leather or fabric on one or both sides of the metal arch.

❑ If the horse is close to a corner and the head and neck are bent back, it may be necessary to first slide it backwards away from the wall, so that he has room to use them to balance and organize himself when rising. Do this by slipping one end of a lunge rein under the neck and through between the front legs; pull on both ends to slide the horse back.

❑ If the bed is very well banked up at the sides, removing some of this bedding may give sufficient room for the horse to regain his feet without further assistance. If not, you will have to roll him over: pass one lunge rein around the fore pastern closest to the ground, and another one around the hind pastern closest to the ground. Be very careful whilst doing this, in particular not to get trapped yourself between the horse and the wall. Do not tie the lunge reins in place.

❑ One person should hold both ends of each lunge line, keeping just enough tension to prevent them from slipping off or moving higher up the legs, whilst the person sitting on the neck gets up and moves to a safe distance.

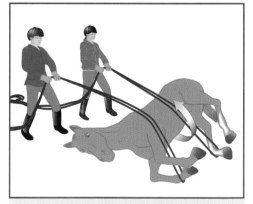

Rolling a cast horse using two lunge reins

❑ Keeping a safe distance from the horse themselves, both the people holding the lunge reins should move backwards, pulling in a synchronized effort so as to avoid twisting the spine more than necessary, so the horse rolls over on to his other side. Do not wrap the lunge reins round the hands.

❑ Once the horse has been rolled over, drop the lunge lines immediately and stand well clear in case the horse leaps to his feet.

❑ When the horse is up, put a headcollar on him, check for injuries, and call a vet if there is any cause for concern.

❑ Even if all appears to be well, you should look in on the horse periodically over the next few hours in case further problems arise.

❑ Once the horse has been freed, he may not always stand immediately, but may spend a moment or two propped on his chest resting. If, after a few minutes, he still makes no effort to rise, or is unable to do so, or struggles, call the vet.

Horse Cast Against a Fence

If the horse has become cast against a fence, it may be easiest and safest to remove the part of the fence he is trapped against. If he goes down in a trailer and becomes stuck, untie his head and remove the breast bar and any partitions that can be moved before attempting to get him on his feet.

Prevention

Try following the code of practice described here as a means of avoiding the problem in the future:

❑ Bank up beds well around the edges to help stop the horse getting too close to the wall.

❑ Ensure the stable is big enough for the horse.

❑ Fit horizontal strips of wood or make grooves along the kicking boards, to give the hooves more purchase, rather than sliding across a smooth surface. The horse will have a chance of being able to push himself away from the wall.

❑ If the horse is inclined to roll following exercise, give him the opportunity to do so in the school or field first, before returning him to the stable.

❑ If the horse has a tendency to roll a lot, check that it is not due to colic (see Colic, page 52), ill-fitting rugs, or itchiness caused by the type of detergent used to wash his stable clothing.

❑ Anti-cast rollers can help, but need very careful fitting if they are not to cause back injuries. A horse can still become cast whilst wearing one.

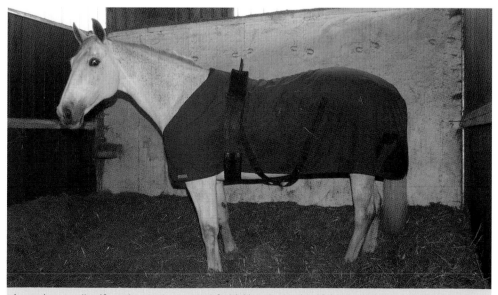

An anti-cast roller, if used, must be a good fit. Making the banks of the bed higher will also help

Legs Caught in Rug Leg Straps

Horses can sometimes get one or both hind legs caught up in the leg straps or crossing surcingles commonly used to help secure rugs in place. This usually happens when the horse lies down if the straps are too slack. The horse may or may not be able to rise.

What To Do

- ❑ If the horse is unable to get up, try to keep him calm and discourage further struggling; kneel or sit on the neck if necessary (see Restraining a Fallen Horse, page 107) and call for help.
- ❑ When this arrives, one person should continue to restrain the horse whilst the other person unfastens the straps, working from the spine side of the horse. It may be necessary to slice through stitching or to cut through the straps themselves if the fastenings have become distorted and cannot be released.
- ❑ Make sure that you both stand well clear as the horse gets up.
- ❑ If he is still unable to rise, call the vet.
- ❑ If the horse is standing with a leg trapped, it may be tempting to deal quickly with the problem yourself; but not so very long ago someone in this situation was kicked in the head and killed. Therefore always call for help instead, and place a headcollar and leadrope on the horse so he can be adequately restrained by one person whilst the assistant unfastens the strap.

Check the fit of your horse's rug. Above: You should be able to get a hand's width between the surcingle and the horse's belly when both straps are done up.
Left: Check that you can get the width of a hand between the horse and the leg strap

Caught Up in a Haynet

Haynets can pose a very real hazard in the stable; if they must be used, it is essential that they are tied at head height to a secure wall ring (never to a piece of twine), and using a quick-release knot (see page 118). Even so, problems can occur: an empty net will dangle much lower than a full one, and drawstrings can fray and break, or may accidentally become untied as the horse picks at the hay. If a net does fall to the floor and the horse's feet become entangled in it, follow the procedure described next.

What To Do

❑ Calm and reassure the horse.
❑ Put on a headcollar and leadrope, and ask someone to hold the horse for you.
❑ Use scissors to cut away the haynet, rather than attempting to untangle the trapped limb(s), as this may frighten the horse more and will only

prolong the process of freeing him. Wear a hard hat, and be very careful as your head will be low and in a vulnerable position if he panics.
❑ Check for injuries; the plasticized nylon mesh can sometimes become deeply embedded.
❑ Occasionally a horse may succeed in hooking up a foreleg in an empty net – usually when the net has not been tied high enough. If this happens, release the net from the wall before attempting to disentangle the leg as above. If the quick-release knot has been pulled immovably tight because of the horse's struggles, or because of the weight of his leg resting in the net, cut the drawstring free.

Feeding Hay

A haynet is not the best way of feeding hay or haylage to horses: it is more natural for them to eat from ground level (as when grazing), for several reasons. First, eating off ground level helps the respiratory system, and it also helps mastication because the teeth align better. When forage is fed from a net, quite apart from the hazard posed by the net itself, digestion tends to be less efficient, and it encourages incorrect musculature and tooth wear. Haynets are helpful in that it is easier to weigh, and/or to soak forage; but whenever possible they should then be emptied onto the floor to be eaten. A haybox can easily be constructed across a corner of the stable to prevent wastage.

If you use a haynet in the stable, rather than feeding from the floor, make sure it is tied at the correct height. The lower edge, when empty, should be no lower than his shoulder

Bridle Caught on a Door Bolt

Never leave a horse loose in the stable with a bridle on, or tied up outside close to the stable door in case the bridle, reins or a bit ring becomes hooked up on the door bolt. The sudden restriction can cause even the most sensible of horses to panic.

What To Do

❑ If it does happen, it may be possible to slide the bridle off, forwards over the ears.
❑ If the horse is leaning back on it too hard to do this, quickly release it by unbuckling a cheekpiece on one side; the bit will drop out of the mouth

and the rest of the bridle will usually come off as the horse then moves rapidly backwards.
❑ Check the mouth carefully for cuts and bruising afterwards, and the bit and bridle for breakages, distortions, and stretched, weakened areas.

Hanging Back Whilst Tied Up

If something startles or scares a horse whilst he is tied up, this can cause him to hang back against the leadrope; and if he does, the sudden poll pressure, the feeling of restriction and of being unable to escape the perceived danger, can then make him panic even more. It is always best to tie a horse to a piece of twine attached to the tie-ring, as the twine is more likely to give way under strain; the ring itself will not, and the horse's struggles may lead to neck injuries or to him losing his footing and falling.

① ② ③ ④ ⑤ ⑥ ⑦ ⑧

How to tie a quick-release knot. Remember what you tie up to is as important as the knot you tie. Use a well fixed wall ring or similar and always use a loop of string. Never attach the rope directly to the ring. If the horse panics, the string should break under the force and free the horse avoiding injury!

What To Do

- ❑ Do not try to pull the horse forward again – he is likely to pull back even more violently.
- ❑ Always tie up using a quick-release knot; do not over tighten it.
- ❑ Tug on the free end of the leadrope to undo the quick-release knot.
- ❑ If a quick-release knot hasn't been used, or the horse's struggles have tightened it so much that it will not undo, cut the string it is attached to.
- ❑ Use a piece of breakable string to tie up to. If you have to use baler twine, weaken it by using only half a strand of it.
- ❑ If the leadrope will not come undone, and you don't have a knife to cut the string, shoo the horse forwards from behind in order to lessen the pressure on his head, whilst calling out for help.
- ❑ If you are using a rope halter instead of a head-collar, make sure that the noseband has been knotted so that it won't tighten.
- ❑ Ask an assistant to hold the horse, rather than tying him up whilst he is being clipped or shod, especially if these are operations that he is inclined to be anxious about.

Do Not:

- ❑ Leave a horse tied up and unattended.
- ❑ Tie a horse directly to a fixed object.
- ❑ Tie him up by the bridle reins.
- ❑ Tie him up in a controller-type headcollar.

Bad to Clip

Good Clipping Practice

- ❑ Always take great care when clipping, even if the horse is known to be good.
- ❑ Make sure your equipment is serviced regularly.
- ❑ Always use a circuit breaker when using mains-operated clippers.
- ❑ Blades should be sharp and correctly tensioned, and the horse clean and dry, otherwise the procedure may cause discomfort, which could lead to him becoming irritable.
- ❑ Arrange for an assistant to hold the horse throughout, rather than tying him up.
- ❑ Bear in mind that, when clipping, you (or the person operating the clippers) are frequently in a vulnerable position, particularly when doing areas around the front of the chest, under the belly and between both front and hind limbs; these are also the places that are most likely to be ticklish or to provoke concern.
- ❑ If a horse is known to be difficult to clip, or starts to become so while you are clipping, then stop, and for the safety of all concerned, arrange for the vet to administer a sedative so the task can be completed with as little trauma as possible.

Removing a Shoe

If a shoe becomes very loose and your farrier cannot come to you at short notice, it may be necessary to remove it yourself in order to prevent it from either being pulled off or twisting round on the foot. If this happens it could cause damage to the hoof or to other limbs, a nail may be driven into the sensitive structures, or it may trip your horse and bring him down.

There is nothing better than practical experience, and it is a good idea to ask your farrier to show you how to hold both the back and the front feet correctly, and also, if possible, for you to remove a shoe under his supervision next time he visits the yard.

Protective Clothing and Tools

Regardless of what your farrier normally wears, use protective clothing yourself when taking off a shoe, including a hard hat, gloves and sturdy boots. You will also need something to protect your legs: maybe your farrier will give you one of his old leather aprons; alternatively a pair of full-length leather chaps makes a good substitute.

You will also need a few shoeing tools: a buffer (kept sharp; a blunt one is worse than useless), a hammer, pincers, and a rasp.

You can either buy your own kit, or your farrier may be prepared to give you a few of his old tools, which will be adequate for your purposes.

How to Remove a Shoe

First, put on your protective clothing, gather your tools together, and ask someone to hold the horse for you on a level, well lit spot.

Removing a shoe from a front foot
- ❑ Lift the hoof, flexing the knee and elbow joint and drawing the limb slightly out to the side.
- ❑ Stand facing the horse's quarters, and place the hoof between your legs just above your knees.

Holding a front foot

Turn your toes and knees inwards slightly to help keep the hoof firmly supported.
- ❑ Remember to bend at your knee and hip joints, but try and keep your back straight.

Removing a shoe from a back foot
- ❑ Pick up the hoof, flexing the hock and stifle joint.
- ❑ Stand facing the tail end of the horse, move the leg backwards and slightly outwards, bring the cannon across your thigh, and settle the hoof just above your knees.
- ❑ Keep your toes and knees turned slightly

Holding a back foot

inwards to support the foot. Do not attempt to hold a back hoof between your legs.

Knocking up the clenches

❑ Place the blade of the buffer under each clench in turn, and tap the blunt, broader side of it fairly boldly until the clench rises upwards, flat to the hoof wall.

❑ If the clenches are very tight and you are having difficulty in lifting them, use the rasp to rasp them off instead.

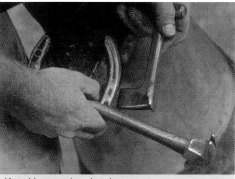

Knocking up the clenches

❑ Next, take the pincers and use them to lever the shoe up at the heels. Lift both heels, then knock the shoe back down again; this will leave the nail heads that lie closest to the heels standing proud.

Using pincers to raise the heels of the shoe

❑ Place the jaws of the pincers around each in turn, and using the shoe for leverage, roll the pincers along the line of the shoe to draw each nail out.

❑ Now lever up the shoe on each side with the pincers to raise the next inner pair of nails, and repeat as before. Work evenly from the heels and round towards the toes.

Nail Pullers

If you know how to use them correctly, nail pullers may be easier, especially with a recently shod foot. Ask your farrier to demonstrate their use.

❑ Don't try to pull the shoe off in one go as your farrier does; most people haven't either the strength or the technique to do so without causing damage to the hoof wall.

❑ Once the shoe has been removed, check the hoof wall for damage and if there are any ragged edges, run the rasp very lightly round them so they do not split further.

❑ If necessary, use a protective boot (such as an Equiboot) to protect the hoof until the farrier can call.

Routine Checks

Check your horse's shoes each day for signs of wear, or if they need re-fitting. Even if the shoes are not badly worn, because the hoof wall continues to grow, re-shoeing will be needed at regular intervals; depending on the individual, the roadwork you do, and the time of the year (feet tend to grow more rapidly during the warmer months in horses out at grass), this should be every 4–6 weeks.

Risen clenches can be very sharp and inflict nasty gashes on the opposite leg. Tap them back down with a hammer, and book your farrier to come and attend to them as soon as he can.

See also:

Aggressive Horses, page 113

Coping with a Cast Horse, page 114

Legs Caught in Rug Leg Straps, page 116

Caught Up in a Haynet, page 116

Horse Rears when Led, page 109

Horse Pulls Away when being Led, page 109

Bucking and Kicking when Turned Out

Some horses will display excitable behaviour, bucking and kicking out, when they are turned out in the field, especially if they have had to wait their turn whilst others are taken out first. A horse may also behave in a lively manner if he has been confined in his stable for a period of time, for example whilst recovering from an injury.

What To Do

❑ To turn out such a horse with the least risk to yourself, you will need the help of a second person to open and shut the gate for you; this is so you can focus your attention on the horse. Leave the gate slightly ajar so you can slip quickly back through it again.

❑ Having led the horse through the gateway, turn him back to face it again. Stand close to the open side of the gate before you remove the head-collar: you can then move quickly through the gap and be safely out of the way of his back feet in the time it takes him to turn around.

Always turn a horse's head to the gate before releasing him

Bullying

Horses that are turned out in a group together usually have a well defined social hierarchy. However, sometimes one of them may be mercilessly bullied by one or more of the others in the group, and this can lead to injury.

Problems Occur:

❑ When two animals are close in status

❑ When a horse has not been well 'socialized'

❑ When grazing is overcrowded and there is greater competition for food

❑ When mares and geldings are grazed together

❑ When constant changes are made to the group of horses

What To Do

❏ Always be careful when introducing a new horse to an already established group; it is best to do this over a period of time, introducing the others to the new horse one by one.

❏ If a horse is seen to be aggressive and bullying the others, remove this one from the field first, and only then go back to rescue the 'victim'; you will then avoid the risk of the bully hassling you whilst you are leading the 'victim' out.

❏ Always carefully monitor any horse turned out with a new group during the first few days.

CASE EXAMPLE

Gentleman Turns Tyrant

A perfect gentleman in most respects, George could be a tyrant when turned out in the field. Despite the other owners at the livery yard complaining about the situation, nothing was done about it – until one day he drove a pony straight through a barbed wire fence. The pony was severely cut, with several serious lacerations requiring extensive stitching. Following this incident, George was removed to an adjacent field on his own. He was checked over by a vet, and found to be a rig (he had not been properly gelded).

Straying

Horses are by nature herd animals, and are happiest when they are with other equines rather than on their own; however, if they are low in the 'pecking order', if forage is in short supply, or in some cases of bullying (see Bullying, page 122), they may either try and escape from, or be driven right out of, the field they are kept in. Horses may also stray if, for example, a footpath runs through the field and walkers fail to secure the gateways, or they may be deliberately let out, or they may push their way out through simple curiosity if the fencing is weak or in poor repair. It is important that you have adequate Third Party insurance; this should cover you for any damage caused by your horse straying, for which you may be held responsible.

Check fencing daily for any parts that need attention; if you come across such a spot and do not have time to repair it there and then, do not turn your horse out in that field until it has been attended to.

Horses that lean on fencing in order to graze the grass on the other side will soon weaken it; some larger horses even learn to lean on it until it gives way. If this is the case, use electric fencing to create an inner margin and prevent this from happening.

Foals may accidentally roll under post-and-rail fencing, and small ponies sometimes learn to do so: the bottom rail should be low enough to ensure this can't happen.

Sometimes a horse learns to 'fence hop', and will make a habit of jumping out of the field: use electric fencing to prevent this, by increasing the height of the existing fence with one line, and using another line on the 'take-off' side to make it wider.

What To Do

- ❑ If you arrive at the field to find that your horse has escaped, contact the police immediately. You might ring the local veterinary practices as well, in case they have been asked to attend to a loose, injured horse.
- ❑ Contact as many friends as possible and organize search parties.
- ❑ Take a headcollar and leadrope and a bucket of food, and look out for any obvious clues as to the direction the horse has taken, such as fresh hoofprints.
- ❑ If you come across a loose horse or horses, be cautious in your approach; they may be in a state of high excitement and easily startled into running off. If they are on or near a road, flag down any passing motorists to assist in directing traffic, and contact the police, and the owner if known.
- ❑ If the horse(s) belongs to you, call for help; aim at keeping them contained, using slow, careful movements with your arms and body until you have more assistance.
- ❑ If there is an empty field or farmyard close by, it may be possible and prudent to herd them into there, safely away from the road, before attempting to catch them.

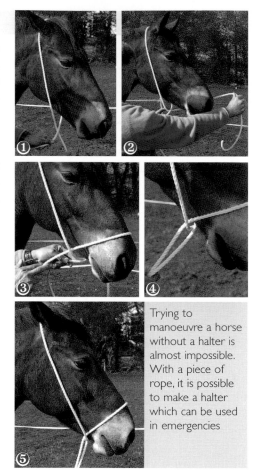

Trying to manoeuvre a horse without a halter is almost impossible. With a piece of rope, it is possible to make a halter which can be used in emergencies

Attacks on Horses

There is increasing concern about the incidence of attacks made on horses by people. These can range from cutting the hair of the mane and tail, to horrific mutilations and sexual assaults; and some of these attacks have proved fatal. It is impossible to make any yard or field 100 per cent secure, but do the best you can (see Security, page 164); and don't assume that attacks will only occur during the dark of night – they can also happen in broad daylight in the middle of the day.

What To Do

If you suspect someone is carrying out an attack, do not put yourself at risk:

❑ Do not approach or try to tackle the person on your own.
❑ Call the police immediately.
❑ Call the vet if necessary.
❑ Note any details that may be helpful, such as the appearance and clothing of the attacker, and the registrations of any strange vehicles parked nearby.

If you discover a horse with injuries that you suspect are from an attack:

❑ Consult the vet; often the injuries are not the result of an attack, but simply traumatic injuries – for example, a wire wound can often look like a knife attack.
❑ If the vet concurs that the injury *is* due to an attack, call the police.
❑ Note any relevant details that may be of help.
❑ Try not to disturb the surrounding area any more than is absolutely necessary, so as not to disturb any possible clues.

Fireworks

Every year there are stories of injuries to both humans and animals caused by fireworks. In the UK, the Fireworks Act is due to become law in time for November 2004, and will hopefully help reduce the extent of the problem, even though it will not completely eliminate it.

Most horses are best kept in secure stabling overnight during the firework 'season', as there is a high risk of them breaking out of their field if they are frightened by the noises and lights. It will also prevent them from becoming victims of deliberate attacks with fireworks.

You may be aware of well advertised public displays being held in the area, but private events can be more difficult to find out about, and are just as likely to cause trouble. Ask neighbours to let you know of any plans they may have, or if they hear of other firework parties that are going to be held in the vicinity; and if you feel they are going to be too close for comfort, consider finding stabling further away for that night.

What To Do

❑ Bring your horse in from the field well before dusk falls – children's parties may start early.
❑ Ensure that sand, water and fire extinguishers are on hand in case of fire (see Fire, page 110, and Fire Prevention, page 166). It is not just fireworks, but stray sparks from bonfires that may pose a fire hazard to the yard.

❑ Provide plenty of hay to keep horses occupied, and check them regularly through the evening. If your horse is likely to become distressed, consult your vet in advance about sedation.
❑ Check the field carefully the next day for any stray fireworks that may have landed there, before turning your horse out.

Suspected Neglect

These cases can often be highly frustrating, both for the person initially reporting the case, and those dealing with it, as it is not always possible to take immediate action. Furthermore, often the cause is in fact ignorance, rather than intentional cruelty, and sometimes for legal reasons nothing can be done beyond warning and advising the owner, and following up with further checks to ensure the situation is being remedied.

What To Do

❑ If you suspect that a horse or pony is suffering from neglect or being ill treated, contact an established equine welfare group.

❑ If you believe the situation to be a real emergency, contact your local police station; they may well be reluctant to deal with it, so you may need to be persistent, but if a formal complaint is lodged they will be obliged to investigate, usually taking along a vet or animal welfare officer.

❑ Provide as much detail as you can, including the owner's name if you know it, the location of the horse, and the nature of the problem.

❑ Ask the organization if they can notify you when they have investigated the matter, and to let you know what action they are going to take.

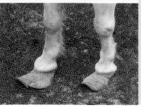

Typical cases of neglect shown in these photographs supplied by The International League for the Protection of Horses (ILPH).

The ILPH, based in the UK, advise the following: If people come across any horses, ponies or donkeys that they think may be suffering they should call the ILPH on the Welfare Line (0870 871 1927). Their suffering could be due to:

❑ lack or absence of water, especially in summer months;

❑ absence of food (ie no grass or hay) which would show in:

❑ poor bodily condition (see top left) – easily visible hips, ribs and spine in the summer months, but not so easily detectable under a thick winter coat;

❑ obviously untreated wounds or skin infections;

❑ excessively overgrown feet (see left)

What Not To Do

❏ Report it to several organizations simultaneously as this can lead to confusion, it wastes resources, and may reduce the chances of a successful outcome.

❏ Attempt to take matters into your own hands, no matter how tempting it may be. If an owner is in fact already under investigation with the possibility of prosecution, and the animal is going to be removed, intervention on your part can undo weeks of work.

❏ Try to remove the animal, since you will be breaking the law yourself and may be charged with theft, no matter how extenuating the circumstances. It is also likely that you will meet with physical resistance from the owner.

Caught Up in a Headcollar

A headcollar should not be left on a horse when he is turned out in the field or left standing loose in the stable, as there is always the risk that he may become hooked up on something. Furthermore, if the horse scratches behind an ear with a back foot, as some do, the hoof may get caught up in it, and the horse could then even fall in its struggle to free himself.

The nylon web headcollars which are commonly used are often so tough as to be virtually unbreakable. A thinner leather headcollar is often more user friendly and will generally break in an emergency.

What To Do

❏ If a headcollar does have to be left on a horse out in the field for some reason, it should be a close fit, and of the type incorporating a 'breakaway' section so that if it becomes snagged on anything, the pressure will cause it to give way and release the horse. Never try to lead a horse in this type of headcollar however, and if left on for any length of time, check it daily for signs of chafing.

❏ If a non-breakaway-type headcollar has been used and the horse has become caught up on an object, take care when approaching him as he may be panicky and could struggle wildly. First, undo the buckle of the headpiece so the horse is released as quickly as possible; he may lunge away the moment he feels he is free, so be ready to move quickly away.

❏ If the buckle has become bent due to the weight of the horse pulling against it, you may be unable to undo it, and you will have to cut through the headpiece. Try to keep the horse from struggling further (see Restraining Horses page 104), and call for assistance.

❏ If the horse has a back foot trapped through a loose-fitting headcollar, release it by undoing the buckle of the headpiece as before, but remain well forward by the side of the head as you do so, in order to avoid injury from the freed foot.

❏ If the horse has fallen with his foot trapped in this manner, approach and release it from behind his head so you will not be injured if he kicks out either during the rescue, or as he gets to his feet again.

Foot Caught in Wire

Wire is an undesirable fencing material for fields grazed by horses, and barbed wire especially is high risk as regards injury. Where there are horses on both sides of a fence they could risk getting a leg caught through it, as they may strike out with a foreleg whilst fraternizing with each other. Sheep netting is no better, as it is possible for a hoof to slip through the mesh and become trapped.

Where a wire fence (of any type) is the only option, it is sensible practice to put up an inner barrier of high visibility electric fencing of design suitable for horses, some five metres from the main fence, as a safety margin.

What To Do

If you find a horse entangled in wire, you should follow this code of procedure:

❑ Call for assistance immediately. You will need at least one other person, equipped with wire cutters, protective clothing for you both, and a headcollar and leadrope if you do not have one with you.

❑ Whilst you are waiting, try to keep the horse as calm and still as possible.

❑ Do not try and extricate a trapped limb by attempting to lift it free; this may make the horse panic even more, causing him to pull back harder or to rear, possibly making matters even worse.

❑ When help arrives, ensure that you each put on hard hats and gloves before attempting to rescue the horse. One person should hold the horse, standing if possible on the same side as the person cutting the wire.

❑ Tautly stretched wire can recoil viciously once the tension is released by cutting, so take care whilst doing this. If a third person is available, they can hold the wire whilst the other person is cutting it, to try and prevent this happening. If the wire has become trapped between the shoe and hoof it will have to be cut on both sides.

❑ At all times be alert for the possibility that the horse may suddenly struggle violently to try and escape the restriction, and be ready to move out of harm's way. Some horses will stand very calmly, but others may explode without any warning at all.

❑ Once the horse is freed, check for injuries and treat accordingly.

❑ Check also that the horse's anti-tetanus vaccinations are up to date.

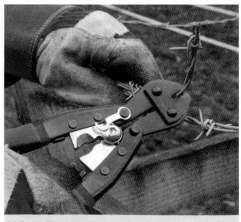

Using wire cutters

Horse Fallen in Ditch

It is not unheard of for a horse to fall in a ditch and get stuck in it, so for safety's sake, any ditch that lies within the field margins should be fenced off.

What To Do

❑ If the horse is upright but can't get out because the sides are too steep, or there isn't enough room to manoeuvre, bales of hay or straw can be used to make a ramp for him to scramble up.

❑ If, however, he is wedged on his back or side, call for assistance immediately as this is an abnormal position, and one that could cause medical problems. A vet will be needed to treat any injuries and possibly to sedate the horse during the rescue operation, and either the Fire Brigade, or someone with a tractor, must be called to winch him out.

❑ Bear in mind that as horses can only breathe through their nostrils, it is quite possible for them to drown in just a few inches of water. If the ditch has water in it, keep his head above it – a bale can be used to prop it up, though take care not to get close to his limbs in case he begins to thrash around in panic.

❑ If a rider is trapped beneath the horse, ring for an ambulance too. In this case it is even more vital to get help as quickly as possible, since crush injuries are quite capable of causing serious, even life-threatening complications.

It may be possible to build a ramp using bales of hay or bedding

Major Disasters

The USA has some of the world's most violent weather; in a typical year it can expect around 10,000 violent thunderstorms, 1,000 tornadoes and at least several hurricanes. It is not surprising, therefore, that the American Association of Equine Practitioners (AAEP) has produced some useful guidelines on how you should prepare for, and cope with, such emergency and disaster situations.

Although the weather in the UK is not generally as severe, heavy rainfall and flooding appear to be on the increase countrywide, and snowfall, certainly in the north of the country, can sometimes cause severe disruption and damage, as can high winds; and even with regular weather warnings, many are caught unprepared. However, it is likely that changes in climatic conditions will increasingly result in weather conditions that are a threat to property and lives.

What To Do

It is important to determine the type of disaster that is most likely to affect you, and to work out a suitable plan of action:

❑ Listen to, and take notice of, any weather warnings, and prepare a kit containing all the things you may need in an emergency, including human and equine first aid kits, plus sufficient supplies of feed and water for 48–72 hours.

❑ Make sure you have a battery recharging kit for your mobile, one that can be plugged into a car cigarette lighter in case of disrupted electricity supplies.

❑ Consider alternative supplies of power in the event of it being cut off, such as a generator.

❑ You may need to evacuate your horse to safer ground, so check out all possible routes to your intended destination, and be sure that transport will be available if required. Have a list of several alternative locations you can take your horse to.

❑ Prepare an ID kit for your horse containing all his details, including special feeding instructions, and information on any medication. Keep his vaccinations up to date; if these have lapsed you might be refused entry to another yard. If you are forced to evacuate, remember to take these records with you.

❑ Develop a 'buddy' system with a friend; you can pool resources, and check on each other before and following a disaster.

❑ The AAEP booklet *Equine Emergency Preparedness* (see Useful Addresses) is full of good advice. There are also many useful websites.

Flash Floods

Always check the most up-to-date weather forecast before hacking out. But even if it seems all right, be aware of the fact that conditions can sometimes change very rapidly, and that it isn't always possible to predict where flooding will occur.

What To Do

If you are unexpectedly caught out in heavy weather, bear in mind the following advice:

❑ Do not cross streams or rivers that are beginning to flow more strongly than usual.

❑ Avoid riding along dry riverbeds that have been caused by previous flash floods.

❑ If flooding begins, move to higher ground; also move stabled horses if buildings are threatened.

Lightning and Thunderstorms

Always check the most recent weather forecast before setting out on a ride; do not go out during a thunderstorm or if one is predicted. Thunderstorms are always accompanied by lightning, and a bolt can deliver one million volts of electricity with a temperature of around 30,000°C. Also other hazardous weather events may be associated with thunderstorms, including flash floods, hailstorms and strong winds.

What To Do

If you are caught out riding in a thunderstorm, try to observe the following code of practice:

❑ Seek safe shelter as quickly as possible.

❑ If you see lightning, count the seconds between seeing the flash and hearing the thunder. The greater the length of time between them, the further away from you is the storm – but still do not delay in seeking safe shelter.

❑ If your horse becomes frightened, try to reassure and calm him. If you are riding, you will need to decide whether it is safer to remain mounted or to lead him instead – whichever gives you adequate control while least endangering you.

❑ Keep away from telephone lines and electricity power lines as these may be struck by lightning and brought down.

❑ Do not take shelter under a tree, as lightning will often strike the highest object around; many people have been killed by lightning flowing through the ground around trees, or by a tree that has been struck and has fallen on them.

❑ Keep away from water, and also metal objects such as wire fences.

❑ Avoid wide open spaces or exposed hilltops.

❑ If your hair begins to stand on end, or nearby objects begin to buzz, move away as fast as you can, as lightning may be about to strike.

❑ If you are caught out in the open and you cannot find any suitable shelter nearby, move towards lower ground.

❑ Note that if a person is struck by lightning, they will have no electrical charge and can be touched safely. Call the appropriate emergency services, and check for respiration and pulse (see Artificial Ventilation, page 158, and Cardio-Pulmonary Resuscitation, page 159).

Breakdowns and Accidents whilst Travelling

The majority of breakdowns involving horse-related vehicles could be prevented if simple regular maintenance procedures were carried out on the horsebox or towing vehicle on a regular basis. Thus regular servicing and safety checks are advisable – in particular if the vehicle has been left unused for a period – by a specialist mechanic. And if buying a secondhand vehicle, even though to your eye it may appear to be in good condition, it is also a wise precaution to have it thoroughly checked over before using it yourself.

Regular maintenance and safety checks are vital if you are to prevent avoidable accidents

What To Do

❑ Join a breakdown scheme that not only provides twenty-four-hour roadside assistance in the event of a breakdown, but also alternative transport for your horse, or overnight stabling if a repair cannot be carried out.

❑ Do not set out in icy weather, especially if you have to drive along ungritted roads; if a trailer or lorry starts to get out of control in such conditions there may be little you can do to stop it. High-sided vehicles are also at risk of being blown over or of veering out of control in strong winds, so avoid travelling in these conditions, too; and if you are inadvertently caught out in them, decrease your speed until you can find a sheltered spot where you can pull over and wait until it has died down.

❑ If using a trailer, first be sure that your towing vehicle is suitable for the laden weight. If you have never towed a trailer before, ask an experienced person to accompany you whilst you practise with an unladen one first.

❑ Anticipate and read the road ahead: allow more time for braking and remember that acceleration will also be much slower. Take care that the engine does not overheat when climbing steep hills; start the ascent in a low-ratio gear if you have it, otherwise engage a low gear.

❑ Many accidents involving trailers are preceded by 'snaking', where it starts swaying from side to side. If this happens, ease off the throttle and slow down gently – don't try to either accelerate or brake hard. Trying to correct the sway with the steering wheel will also make matters worse, so try to hold the wheel straight ahead until the snaking stops.

❑ If the trailer begins to tip over, steer at once into the direction it is tilting to try and bring it back on to its wheels.

❑ In the event of a breakdown, move the vehicle over to the hard shoulder or side of the road if possible. Switch on the hazard lights and place warning triangles on the road so as to warn other drivers, and contact your breakdown service.

❑ Check on the horse(s) whilst awaiting rescue, but do not attempt to unload them.

❑ Once the breakdown service has arrived you will be able to determine whether a roadside repair can be effected; if it cannot, and you have to transfer the horse to another vehicle, there will be more hands available to do this safely.

❑ If you do have an accident, switch off the engine ignition. Use the vehicle hazard lights, and set up warning triangles to alert other drivers.

❑ Check for, and assess human and equine casualties, and take appropriate action: seek assistance from other motorists with the casualties and also with traffic control, if possible.

❑ Call for the emergency services as required.

Use hazard lights and warning signs to alert other motorists if you break down

Road Traffic Accidents

What To Do

Should you be present at a road traffic accident involving a horse or pony, your first priorities must be to control the injured animal, and to direct the traffic so that further accidents are not caused.

❑ Enlist the aid of passing motorists or pedestrians, and delegate as much as possible, since you cannot be everywhere at once: they can help with traffic control, deal with human casualties, and alert the emergency services, and if necessary can be shown how to hold or restrain the injured horse safely should your assistance be required more urgently elsewhere at the scene.

❑ If possible, move the horse off the road away from other traffic. If, however, the horse is down and it is clear he either cannot or will not get up, he may be badly hurt, so do not force him to move.

If he thrashes around attempting to rise but is clearly unable to do so, be prepared to restrain him by kneeling on his neck (see Restraining a Fallen Horse, page 107).

❑ Set up warning posts 200m (250yds) both ahead and behind the accident area. Make sure that the ignition of any damaged vehicle is switched off, and also the fuel supply on motorcycles.

❑ Attend to human casualties, and ring the police and any other emergency services as required (see Making Emergency Calls, page 102).

❑ Do not get involved in arguments or accusations, but concentrate on dealing with the situation in hand; keep others occupied if possible.

❑ Try to memorize the incident if you saw what actually happened.

Horse Refuses to Load

This can be a most frustrating problem. Very often it is due to a previous bad experience – about which the owner may be completely ignorant – and is best dealt with slowly, re-educating the horse to help him overcome his fears. However, until he will load reliably, it is best not to travel him unless absolutely essential.

If you really do have to travel a poor loader – for example, to the vet – leave plenty of time, and if you find yourself running behind schedule, phone them to tell them, and phone them again once you are on your way so you can provide an estimated arrival time. In this situation it is essential to take an assistant with you.

What To Do

Try the following procedure:

❑ First, park the vehicle so that the interior is as well lit as possible. Use interior lights if available, or leave the front ramp of a front-unload trailer down. Do not open the groom's door as there have been instances of horses trying to escape through this and becoming wedged in the process.

❑ Some horses may find a steep ramp difficult to negotiate, so use a gradient if one is available to help decrease the height. Lay down bedding both inside the vehicle and on the ramp to help make it more inviting. Move the partitions across where possible, to give more space.

❑ Do not lose your temper or shout at the horse, as this creates more stress for all involved, and the horse may be even less likely to load. Never try to ride the horse into the vehicle.

❑ Do not keep constantly pulling on the headcollar and leadrope, as the restriction will cause the horse to pull back harder, or possibly to rear. Use food to tempt the horse forwards, and use the verbal command 'Walk on'.

❑ Have an assistant pick up the horse's feet in turn and move them forwards. Pause for a moment or two after each foot is moved. The helper should take care in case the horse suddenly moves sideways, backwards, kicks or rears.

❑ If the front feet are on the ramp, but the back

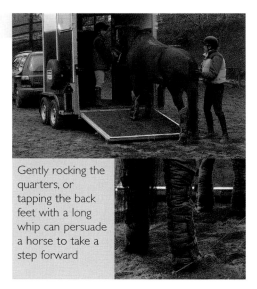

Gently rocking the quarters, or tapping the back feet with a long whip can persuade a horse to take a step forward

feet have become planted, try tapping each of the hooves in turn with the end of a long whip, or very gently rocking the quarters with a hand on the hip to restore body awareness and movement. Take care in case the horse kicks out. Try tapping the rump with a long whip, again taking care not to get within kicking distance. Do not use the whip aggressively or excessively: if a smart tap has no effect, neither will a beating.

❑ If all else fails, take two lunge lines and securely attach one line to each side of the rear of the vehicle. Have one person hold the end of each line, thus forming a wide enclosure at the foot of the ramp: lead the horse into this. As he moves forwards, each person moves across to the opposite side so that the lines cross behind the hindquarters, thus encouraging the horse forwards from behind. (Note that everyone should wear a hard hat, sensible footwear and gloves.) The two assistants at the rear should be directed by the person leading the horse as to when to exert a little pressure, and when to cease it. The lines must not be allowed to slip up beneath the horse's dock as this may cause him to panic; nor should they be allowed to slide downwards on to the hamstrings.

❑ If the horse attempts to rear or run backwards, the lines should both be released so that pressure from them does not push the hindlimbs so far forward beneath the horse that he becomes unbalanced and falls.

❑ This is a technique that should only be attempted by those who have had experience of using it before.

Using lunge reins to encourage a reluctant loader

Traffic Shy

A horse that is apprehensive and nervous on the roads should not be taken out on them; they are dangerous enough even for a reliable horse. Even with a confident horse you may occasionally meet a vehicle that is unfamiliar to it, and which he finds frightening; or with the best intentions a lorry driver will brake to slow down to pass you, but in doing so the sharp hiss of the released air pressure will alarm the horse.

What To Do

If your horse shows anxiety at the approach of a vehicle observe the following code of practice:

❑ Remain mounted, as you will have more control.

❑ Use verges, or move into a gateway, drive or road junction if there is one, until the vehicle has passed.

❑ If there is no immediate gateway or suchlike in which to take refuge, ask the vehicle to slow down until you have reached one; or if it is an oncoming vehicle, to stop until you are past it. If you cannot take a hand off the reins, mime the words 'Stop, please'.

❑ Keep the horse flexed in the direction of the centre of the road (or away from the vehicle), and use plenty of inside leg at the same time to maintain control and prevent the quarters from swinging into the path of traffic.

Broken Stirrup Leather

It is always a good idea to buckle a sound stirrup leather around the neck of your horse before going out on a ride (see also What to Take on a Ride, Part 4 page 179); this will double as a neckstrap as well as a spare leather in case of emergencies.

What To Do

❑ If a stirrup leather breaks whilst out hacking, and you do not have a spare one with you, it may still be possible to use it on a higher hole. Make sure you shorten the other stirrup leather to the same length so that you are not riding lopsidedly, as this will have an adverse effect on your balance. Remain in walk whilst you return home so that you do not place undue stress on the broken leather.

❑ If the leather has given way due to worn or rotted stitching, rather than breaking at a hole, it is safest to dismount and remove it, then run up the opposite stirrup iron and lead your horse home. It may be tempting to ride without stirrups, but this is not a safe practice; if something unexpected happens causing your horse to spook or misbehave you may become unseated.

Broken Girth Strap

It is usually a girth strap that breaks, or one of the webs to which it is attached, rather than the girth itself. The girth should always be buckled to girth straps that are stitched to two separate webs, so that should one fail, the other will hopefully hold the saddle secure until the problem is discovered.

Attach the girth to straps stitched to separate webs

What To Do

❑ If you find that one strap or web has broken, stop immediately: do not attempt to ride on just one.
❑ If a third girth strap is present, the girth can be buckled to this as a temporary measure to enable you to return home (in walk) if out on a ride. It should then be sent for repair – don't just continue to use the extra strap instead, as it will affect the way the saddle sits and may cause discomfort or lead to slipping (see Saddle Slips, page 137). Before using the third girth strap, always check it very carefully first; bear in mind that if the breakage was due to poor maintenance or wear and tear, the other straps may be in a similar condition. If you have any doubt as to its integrity, run up the stirrups and lead the horse home.

❑ If you are unlucky enough to have both girth straps or webs fail, it is likely to result in a fall, as the saddle is then bound to part company unexpectedly with the horse (see Falling Off, page 139).

Broken Rein

What To Do

❑ Should a rein break whilst you are riding, use a verbal command to the horse, to slow down or halt. Quick, rapid, upward tugs on the neckstrap (see What to Take on a Ride, Part 4 page 179) may also help slow him down, and use the rein you still have to give a series of half halts.

❑ Kick both feet free of the stirrups and jump off as soon as the horse's speed has decreased sufficiently to allow you to do so safely, and then bring him to a halt. If he will not slow down sufficiently, use the unbroken rein to bring him round into an ever-decreasing circle until he does (though take care not to pull him round sharply, as this will unbalance him and may cause him to fall).

❑ If circling is not an option due to lack of space in which to do so safely, hold the unbroken rein and a handful of mane in the same hand to help keep you balanced, then push your lower legs forward slightly, keeping the heels deep, and reach forward with your free hand to take hold of the dangling section of rein, the bit ring or bridle cheekpiece. Use this in combination with the good rein to slow the horse down or to stop him.

Saddle Slips

This may be due to poor conformation, poor saddle fit, or if the girth is too loose; it can also occur when tackling steep gradients. It can be frightening for the horse, and the movement and discomfort may lead to a panic reaction such as bucking or bolting.

What To Do

❑ If you feel the saddle slip, even slightly, do not attempt to continue, but slow down and get off.

❑ Stop or at least slow the horse sufficiently to be able to dismount safely.

❑ Take both feet out of the stirrups and dismount.

❑ Keep hold of the reins as you do so. If the horse has not halted completely but is still moving forward, remember to keep moving forwards with him as your feet touch the ground, otherwise you will lose your balance and may fall over.

❑ If the saddle has slipped to one side, dismount on the side to which the saddle has slipped.

❑ Halt the horse if he has not already halted himself. Speak reassuringly to him, and cross the stirrup leathers and irons over the seat of the saddle so they do not swing and frighten him.

❑ Undo the girth, and remove the saddle carefully. If it has slipped to one side, unbuckle the girth on that side. If the horse is anxious it may not stand still; if someone is available to help, ask them to hold it whilst you attend to the saddle.

❑ If for some reason you are unable to support the saddle as you unbuckle the girth straps and it falls to the ground, be aware of the fact that the horse is likely to swing sideways away from it. Afterwards it is important to ask your saddler to check the saddle fit; also whether it would be advisable to use a crupper or a breastgirth; and which girth straps to attach the girth to in order to help minimize any undesirable movement.

❑ Check the girth before and after mounting, and again after you have ridden for ten minutes.

Horse's Tongue over the Bit

Some horses will become extremely anxious if they get their tongue over the bit. The rider's control is severely compromised as the horse's anxiety gets the better of him, often causing him to throw his head up violently, thereby losing his balance and compromising his awareness of other objects around.

What To Do

- ❑ Lengthen the reins: a stronger contact will just make the situation worse – the horse may panic and rear or run backwards.
- ❑ Dismount immediately.
- ❑ Leave the reins around the horse's neck.
- ❑ Unbuckle the bridle cheekpiece closest to you to lower the bit from the horse's mouth.
- ❑ Use the reins around its neck to maintain control whilst you replace the bit and rebuckle the cheekpiece.
- ❑ As soon as possible, check for cuts and bruising in the mouth under the tongue and on the bars.
- ❑ Make sure that the mouthpiece of the bit is not excessively wide or hanging too low in the mouth, as this will increase the likelihood of the tongue being displaced over it. If the horse is inclined to do this regularly, get the teeth checked and ask your instructor for advice on the horse's bitting arrangements, and whether your riding has anything to do with the problem.

Horse's Foot over the Rein

This particular dilemma often happens when the horse is allowed to graze with a bridle on, either when being led or ridden; it is therefore important always to keep a careful eye on where the reins are in relation to the horse's head at such moments, and never allow them to become completely slack.

What To Do

- ❑ If the horse puts a foot over one of the reins whilst you are mounted, dismount immediately.
- ❑ Either lift the hoof back over the rein again, or slide the reins up to the chest and unbuckle them, taking care not to allow the ends to dangle on the ground, where they may be trodden on.
- ❑ If the horse has actually trodden on the rein with a forefoot, lift the hoof to release the rein. If it is straining its head upwards against the pressure on its mouth it may find it hard to do this – should this be the case, try grasping the fetlock or pastern and sliding the hoof slightly forwards first before lifting the foot. Be careful as you do so in case it rears as the pressure on its mouth is removed.

Falling Off

In the course of your riding career there are bound to be times when you fall off. Sometimes it seems to happen almost in slow motion, on other occasions it is all so fast and unexpected that you are hardly aware of what has happened until you suddenly find yourself on the ground.

In some situations determination and willpower, combined with an iron grip, will keep you on board, but this isn't always enough – and once you have reached the point of no return, there is little you can do except try and minimize the risk of injury to yourself. This may sound simple, but in practice it isn't quite so easy because you need to override instinctive reactions, such as bracing yourself for impact, or putting out a hand to try and save yourself.

What To Do

If the worst happens and you find yourself parting company with your horse, remember to:

❑ Relax as much as possible.

❑ Try to curl up and roll away from the horse to avoid injury from its hooves.

❑ Tuck your head in against your shoulder, and tuck in your arms and legs to help protect both limbs and internal organs.

❑ Let go of the reins; keeping hold of them can cause you to be dragged along beside your horse, and can lead to a fractured or dislocated shoulder. Being so close to it, you are also in a very vulnerable position, and more likely to get trodden on – and if the restriction causes it to panic, it may well kick out in fear.

❑ If other horses are following along behind, don't try and stand up again immediately, but stay put so they have a chance to avoid you – if you get up and stagger straight into their flight-path they will have even less time to swerve, and will just knock you straight back down again.

Getting Dragged

Probably one of the nastiest and most frightening scenarios is that of a rider falling off, getting a foot trapped in a stirrup and then being dragged by the horse. Quite apart from any injury caused by the fall itself, the horse may well panic and try to gallop away from this frightening object on the ground, often bucking and kicking out at the same time.

There is little that either rider or onlookers can do until either the trapped foot comes free, or the horse stops. Chasing after a horse in this situation may only make things worse, as it is likely to increase its panic; instead you will have to find other ways to persuade it to stop – for instance, the presence of another horse just walking quietly around may help to reassure it and 'draw' it.

Above all, minimize the chances of this sort of thing happening by observing the following code of practice:

❑ Check that the movable thumbpieces on the end of the stirrup bars have been pushed into the 'down' position, so that in most instances the stirrup leather can slide free.

❑ Use safety stirrup irons (right) – several different patterns are available.

❑ Stirrup irons should be 1in (2.5cm) wider than the broadest part of the foot. If they are wider than this, the feet may slide through and become trapped; if they are narrower, the feet may become tightly wedged.

❑ Wear appropriate footwear.

❑ Never place a child's foot through the stirrup leather above the iron when giving a ride.

❑ Punch more holes in long stirrup leathers rather than twisting them around the top of the stirrup iron to shorten them, as this will cause them to hang at an incorrect angle, which will increase the possibility of a foot getting trapped.

❑ Teach the exercise used by the Tellington Touch Equine Awareness Method (TTEAM) (see page 188) called 'sliding numnahs' to your horse where the horse is taught to stand calmly while something slips from his back. One of its useful applications is that in the event of the rider falling off, the horse learns not to be fearful, and to stop rather than run away.

The sliding numnahs exercise is worth teaching

Getting Back On

Despite the traditional advice that stresses the importance of getting straight back on again after a fall, this is not always the best idea.

❑ Before remounting you should first consider why you fell off, so you can avoid repeating the circumstances that led to it. If it was because the horse misbehaved, it may be advisable to enlist the help of an instructor to resolve the problem, rather than inviting further risk to the rider, and perhaps establishing undesirable behaviours in the horse.

❑ Bear in mind also that even if a rider appears otherwise unhurt, if the head has received a blow of any kind, it should be checked out at a hospital; and if concussion is suspected, the rider should absolutely not be allowed to remount. If there is any doubt at all on the matter, it is best to err on the side of caution. A rider who is concussed may:

• experience dizziness;

• feel nauseous;

• have a headache;

• suffer some degree of memory loss;

• appear vague or confused.

Although there is generally a brief period of unconsciousness, concussion can occur without any loss of consciousness, and since all head injuries are potentially dangerous and the level of severity of concussion can sometimes be difficult to assess, medical attention should always be sought. If, following a fall – and even after an apparent full recovery – a rider experiences persistent headaches, memory impairment or difficulty in concentrating, further medical advice should be sought.

After an episode of concussion, it is important to follow medical advice regarding how long to delay before resuming riding activities: in the event of a mild concussion this may be only a week, and in more severe cases it may be as long as seven weeks. (See also Part 3 First Aid for People, page 153.)

Gaining Confidence

Even a minor fall can shake your confidence quite considerably, especially as you grow older or if you have a vivid imagination, when it can alert you to the very real potential for serious physical damage. For most people, falling off doesn't happen that frequently, and when it does, it results in no more than a few bruises and grazes. But whilst these heal quickly, the psychological consequences can very often linger on, and the resulting anxiety that may be experienced on future occasions can do much to spoil the enjoyment of riding, and could even lead to a further, quite unnecessary fall, as rider position will invariably deteriorate due to tension.

Sometimes regaining confidence following a fall can take time, and it may be helpful to seek advice and assistance:

❑ Book some lessons with a good instructor who is sympathetic to your problem, and who will be able to offer constructive help in overcoming your fears.
❑ You could try neuro-linguistic programming (NLP) techniques.
❑ Return to basics, repeating and establishing earlier and simpler work that you know is well within the abilities of both you and your horse.
❑ Try riding a different, steady and quiet horse for a while.

Prevention

Falling off may be an inevitable risk when riding, but you can take steps to try and reduce the likelihood as much as possible:

❑ Improve your position: a correct position increases your ability to communicate with and control your horse, and gives an increased degree of security.
❑ Observe safe and sensible riding practices.
❑ Keep your wits about you at all times when riding, concentrating on what your horse is doing, rather than the latest bit of gossip!
❑ Do not attempt more than you (or your horse) are ready for.
❑ Ensure that your tack is in good repair, well maintained and correctly adjusted.
❑ As you can't plan for a fall, always wear suitable protective clothing when mounted.

Even the most remote country lane is rarely traffic-free. Don't slop along, chatting, in a disorganized group. Keep alert at all times

Horse Rolls with Rider

There are several reasons why a horse might try to roll with its rider still 'on board': some may do this when they are sweaty, if they are working on a surface they are not used to – for example, a schooling arena – or when they are being asked to negotiate water, such as a water obstacle on a cross-country course or a stream, especially if they are inexperienced. Others may actually learn to go down and roll as a way of ridding themselves of their rider, and this can be a very difficult tendency to cure. Rolling may also be due to colic (see Colic, page 52).

This may be an entertaining sight for any onlookers, but it can have really serious consequences should the rider become trapped and crushed beneath the horse; and if the horse rolls on the saddle, it may also damage the tree, and/or sustain back injuries.

What To Do

There are certain definite signs that a horse is about to roll: it will stop, and lower its head to inspect the ground; it will start to paw vigorously with its front hooves; and its front legs will start to buckle at the knees.

If this starts to happen, you may be able to prevent it by:

❏ Maintaining a positive rein contact, trying to keep its head up; this will make it more difficult – though not impossible – for it to go down.

❏ Riding forwards briskly, using legs, voice and if necessary, a smack from the whip.

If you cannot prevent it:

❏ Quickly take both feet out of the stirrups.

❏ Dismount on the side to which the shoulder is dropping.

❏ Move up towards the horse's head so you are out of the way of its hooves. Keep hold of the reins if possible so you can prevent them from becoming entangled round its feet.

Horse Falls

Steep, slippery and unlevel surfaces or deep going can cause your horse to fall, so such terrain should be tackled with care. Tarmac roads can also be extremely slippery.

What To Do

❏ It is best to allow the horse a loose rein so it can use his head and neck to best effect to balance himself. Try to sit in a good balance yourself; also take your feet out of the stirrups as a precaution.

❏ Do not hurry it; allow it to pick its way slowly and carefully in its own time. When tackling a gradient, whether up or down, try to keep as straight a line as possible; moving at an angle to it increases the likelihood of slipping. Use the mane or a neckstrap to help keep yourself balanced, rather than the reins, so you do not restrict the horse's head and neck.

❑ If the ground is very steep, or treacherous, or unstable, dismount and lead the horse: it will find it easier to balance without a rider, and if it does fall, you will be in less danger.

❑ If the horse does begin to fall, jump off as quickly as possible and move out of range of its hooves. Allow it to regain its feet on its own, move to a safer area, and check it for injuries.

Taking Precautions

There are certain precautions you can take to avoid the likelihood of the horse falling.

❑ For instance, when the weather is bad, avoid riding out on roads that are still icy. Snow can pack into the horse's hooves, creating icy 'stilts' that will make it very hard for it to keep its balance. Greasing its soles beforehand may help prevent this to a certain extent, but preferably try to avoid riding in such conditions. Also avoid steep gradients when it is very wet.

❑ Metalled roads can have slippery areas (watch out for worn, shiny patches), so ride close to the kerb where the grip may be slightly better, and use the verge where it is possible and safe to do so. Make sure the horse is shod regularly: shoes that are thin and have worn smooth will increase the likelihood of your horse slipping, especially on metalled roads.

❑ Ask your farrier about the use of studs, or frost nails in the horse's shoes.

❑ If tackling loose surfaces such as shale, it is always better to dismount and lead the horse. Be careful, too, when riding on mossy ground or wet grass, as these can often pose a treacherous surface. And keep an eye out for any potholes or boggy areas that may cause your horse to stumble or trip.

❑ Do not ride through water at speed, as the drag on the horse's legs may cause it to fall. Riverbeds can also be slippery underfoot, and there may be potholes you cannot see.

❑ Always put protective boots on your horse (see Protective Equipment for Horses, page 172).

❑ Be especially careful if your horse is arthritic: if it lacks flexibility in the joints it will be more likely to stumble or fall, especially at speed.

Horse Trapped in a Fence

If a horse becomes stuck or trapped in a fence during the cross-country phase of a competition, there will nearly always be assistance immediately to hand; additional help is likely to be required, however, and should be requested immediately by radio or telephone. Stewards on the earlier part of the course should be instructed to stop other riders before they reach the problem area. Where the rider has also become trapped, priority must always be given to him/her.

What To Do

❑ Restrain the horse's head (see Restraining Horses, page 104). Sometimes offering food helps to keep it calm; if it is thoroughly upset it may help to put on a blindfold. The course vet may have to give the horse a sedative.

❑ If possible, remove the saddle; if not, loosen the girth and run up, or preferably remove the stirrup irons and leathers altogether.

❑ Replace the bridle with a headcollar; this is less likely to slip off or break, especially if traction has to be applied to the head. A lunge line should be attached to the headcollar.

❑ Actually removing the horse from the fence should not be attempted without professional help and equipment, when the best method of achieving this can be determined. It is generally easiest and safest to dismantle the fence, either completely or partially. This may be sufficient for the horse to extricate himself; otherwise he will have to be helped out using ropes. This should all be organized under the direction of the course vet.

❑ Nowadays the use of 'frangible pins' means that the fence is more likely to come apart anyway should a horse collide with it, so the likelihood of it getting stuck is much less.

Lost Whilst out on a Ride

It is a sad fact that if you find yourself lost whilst out hacking, you should be careful about approaching strangers to ask for directions, no matter how normal they appear to be. Remember to carry a map and your mobile phone.

What To Do

❑ If you spot a public telephone box, check inside, as there may be information displayed that will help you to pinpoint your location.

❑ If you are exploring a new area, make sure you carry a sufficiently detailed map with you; in remote areas, take along a compass too. Dismount if you need to check a map as attempting it whilst on horseback may spook your horse.

❑ Along your route note landmarks, road signs and any road names. If you become lost you will then be able to retrace your footsteps if necessary, returning the way you came.

❑ If you do not have a compass with you, note the position of the sun and the time of day; if you know where east and west are, you can also work out where north and south lie, and this will help give you some idea of the approximate direction you need to head in.

❑ If you become lost due to the weather closing in and visibility becoming poor, do not keep going, but stay where you are until you can see where you are going properly again.

❑ If you need to call for help – in a very remote

You should dismount to check a map. While you are busy working out where to go next, your horse may be busy looking for trouble

and isolated area, for example – give as much detail about your location as possible, including any nearby landmarks. Do not wander around whilst waiting for assistance to arrive, as this will make it more difficult for a rescue party to find you.

See also
❑ What to Take on a Ride, page 179
❑ Safe Hacking, page 178

Encountering an Aggressive Person

If you meet anyone who approaches you in an aggressive manner (or who sexually exposes themself to you) whilst out on a ride, do not assume that because you are mounted on a horse you will be safe but be as wary as if you were on foot. There have in the past been incidents where riders have been verbally abused, physically intimidated, and even threatened with firearms. In one recent encounter, an owner leading her horse from the field to its stable for the night was stabbed by a stranger who accosted her; she subsequently died as a direct result of the injuries she received.

What To Do

❑ Try to avoid direct eye contact.
❑ Put distance between yourself and the person as quickly as possible: if riding, do not get close enough for the person to grab the reins.
❑ Do not respond in kind to verbal abuse; it is more likely to inflame the situation.
❑ Report the matter to the police as soon as you possibly can.

Chased by a Dog

The situation of being chased usually occurs when a dog has slipped out from a farmyard or house that you are passing; once you have moved a certain distance away, the dog will usually lose interest and return to guarding its 'territory'.

What To Do

❑ If you are chased by a dog whilst out on a ride, provided your horse is calm and you are able to control him, keep going at a slow but steady pace away from it.
❑ If your horse starts to become anxious, do not dismount, but turn it to face the dog so that it can clearly see it, and try to persuade your horse to stand still until the dog either loses interest or is retrieved by the owner.
❑ If you find a loose dog chasing your horse out in the field, try to remain calm. If the owner is nearby you will both be concerned – you for your horse, and the dog owner for their pet. If you begin shouting at the dog, or try to chase after it to recapture it, the situation will simply get worse, and if you start running around the field, you will both be at risk; very often it ends with the dog being kicked by the horse. However if things have not reached this point, persuade the owner to call encouragingly to the dog whilst moving briskly in the opposite direction so that its attention is drawn away from the horse and to the fact that its owner is leaving.

Horse goes Lame when Hacking

What To Do

❏ If your horse suddenly goes lame whilst you are out hacking, move to a safe area away from any passing traffic, and dismount. Take the reins over his head and run up the stirrups whilst you check him over; if you are with a friend, ask them to dismount and hold both horses while you carry out your investigation.

❏ Unless the cause of the lameness is immediately apparent, start with the obvious: check that it is not due to a stone becoming lodged in a foot. Then check down the legs for signs of cuts, heat, swelling or tenderness; it might well have struck into itself, perhaps into the heel of a front foot, or have sustained a brushing injury, or a sprain.

❏ If you cannot find anything, try walking the horse forward again for a few steps to see if the lameness was perhaps caused by momentary discomfort from standing on a stone.

❏ Depending on what you discover, how far you are from home, and the degree of lameness, either lead your horse back home, or ring for help to collect your horse in a trailer or lorry.

See also
❏ Wounds, page 32
❏ Lameness, page 40
❏ Azoturia, page 64

Horse in Difficulty in Water

Horses may get into difficulty in water in a variety of circumstances, such as falling or slipping into a river where the banks may be too steep to climb out again, venturing on to frozen expanses of water and falling through the ice, and when swimming with their owners in the sea.

If you are going to need assistance in recovering a horse from such a situation, first call the emergency services; then you should contact a vet, as sedation may be required to facilitate the horse's rescue, as well as to give treatment afterwards. Above all, remember not to place yourself at risk whilst waiting for help to arrive; do only as much as you can attempt safely.

Horse in a Swimming Pool

❏ Very occasionally a horse may escape and fall into a swimming pool, and in this case the rescue process can be complicated by the fact that heavy lifting machinery can sometimes be necessary and access to the pool may be limited. However, it is possible to improvise a ramp out of bales of

hay or straw, and often the horse will successfully scramble up this.

❏ Otherwise call for help, and whilst waiting, if it is safe to do so, try to encourage the horse to move towards the shallow end. It may also be necessary to begin draining the pool.

Swimming in the Sea

❑ It can be easy to over-exert a horse when swimming for pleasure in the sea; in a hydrotherapy pool where the horse is being closely monitored all the time, it is estimated that eight laps of a 34m-diameter pool is equivalent to a mile-long gallop. So if swimming with your horse, take care not to overdo things, or to swim so far out from land that returning may be a struggle. Boots should be fitted to the horse's legs to minimize the risk of injury from his exaggerated swimming stroke; a rider should remain on the horse's back so as not to be injured by the limbs.

❑ Before you venture into the sea with your horse, check the time of the tides, and take local advice as to potential hazards such as areas of quicksand on the beach, or rip currents: the latter can happen in all sorts of weather and on a wide range of beaches, and whilst some are just brief occurrences, others are a characteristic of the area. Basically a rip current is a narrow, powerful current of water that runs at a right angle to the land out into the ocean; it can move fairly fast, as its name would imply, and should you find your horse caught in one, do not waste energy trying to swim head on against it towards the shore, but try to guide your horse to swim parallel to the shoreline until you are free of it, and then head back towards land.

Rescuing a Horse from a River or Pond

❑ If the weather is cold, it is important to try and get the horse out as quickly as possible because of the risk of hypothermia. It may be possible to wade out close enough to put on a headcollar and attach a lunge line to encourage the horse to move to another spot where either the water is shallower, or the banks are low enough for it to be able to scramble out; or use food as a lure. As the horse jumps out, keep well clear of him as it may flounder about with its front legs, especially if the ground is slippery.

❑ If a horse has ventured out on to an area of frozen water and has fallen through the ice, do not attempt to go near it as there is a danger that you too may fall through: it is best to wait until help arrives.

Horse Loses a Shoe

Deep going can loosen or suck off a shoe, even if the horse has been recently shod.

You will often hear a clanking noise when riding on a hard surface if a shoe is loose.

What To Do

❑ If you notice that a shoe has become very loose, or that you have lost one altogether, dismount and lead the horse home so as not to risk injury or damage to the foot.

❑ For safety's sake, take the reins over your horse's head and run the stirrups up; depending how far you are from home and how loose the shoe is, either lead him home or call for transport. If you have to lead him and he has lost the shoe, use grass verges where it is possible and safe to do so, to minimize damage to the hoof.

Horse Stuck in a Bog

Some places are notorious for the presence of bogs or quicksand. If you are unfamiliar with the region, take local advice as to the areas that are best avoided, and what to look out for that would indicate a boggy spot; if possible, take a guide with you who knows the locality well. Stick to used tracks where possible, and on open ground look for changes in the vegetation that may warn you of the presence of bogs or quicksand.

What To Do

❑ Be prepared to trust your horse's judgement if he suddenly shows reluctance to move forward; dismount and test the ground ahead.

❑ If you do stumble into a boggy area and the horse begins to sink in even a little, briskly encourage him to extricate itself.

❑ If he continues to sink and is unable to pull himself free, dismount quickly. Keep your body as horizontal as possible so as to spread your weight, and make slow movements to bring yourself to the edge of the boggy ground.

❑ Ring for assistance to help free the horse; try to reassure and calm him with your voice, because if he continues to struggle he will only sink in deeper.

Horse Trapped in a Cattle Grid

A cattle grid is not a suitable 'barrier' for keeping horses contained in a field, and should be fenced or gated off. If there is a cattle grid across a track or road alternative access via a gate at the side will be provided. The gate should be hinged on the grid side so that the gate forms a barrier between the grid and the horse whilst the latter is passing through the gateway; but as you turn to shut the gate behind you, there may still be a danger of the horse stepping sideways and a foot becoming trapped in the grid. It is therefore a sensible precaution to dismount to do this, keeping yourself between the horse and the grid.

If a horse does become trapped in a grid, there is a grave risk of serious injury. There is usually little you can helpfully do beyond calling for help immediately – you will almost certainly require the services of a vet and maybe the fire brigade (hence the importance of carrying a mobile phone) – and trying to keep the horse as calm as possible whilst awaiting their arrival.

Rearing

This is both frightening and dangerous behaviour; if the horse goes up high or is unbalanced by the rider it may fall over backwards crushing him, causing serious injury or even death. Never be persuaded to ride a horse that is known to rear.

What To Do

If a horse does rear up with you, try to do the following:

- ❑ Allow the reins to go completely slack.
- ❑ Stay well forward with your upper body.
- ❑ Put your arms around the horse's neck to help keep yourself forward and in balance.
- ❑ Do not pull on the reins as this can pull the horse over backwards.
- ❑ As soon as the front feet touch the ground again, ride briskly forwards using light but quick leg aids and with the lightest of rein contacts possible.
- ❑ If the horse threatens to rear again, if you have time, kick your feet free of the stirrups and jump off. Do not ride the horse again until you have discussed the matter with an experienced instructor or trainer.

Rearing is both frightening and dangerous

Bucking

Although a few horses may buck out of sheer high spirits if they are overfresh, this behaviour is more usually a response to pain or discomfort, and if it occurs and there is no immediately obvious cause (such as a horsefly bite), it should always be investigated further.

Unless you have a very deep and secure seat – or if the horse bucks very hard – it is easy to become unseated. However, you do sometimes have warning of what is about to happen – namely the head may begin to lower, and the back muscles will start to lift and bunch up – and you can then take quick action to try and stop the horse bucking.

See also
❑ Falling Off, page 139

What To Do

- ❏ Try to keep the horse's head up by raising both your hands.
- ❏ Ride the horse positively forwards into the rein contact.
- ❏ If the horse does buck, try to adopt the following 'safety measures':
  - • Keep both your heels well down and move your lower legs forwards so you are not thrown forwards.

- • Do not lean forwards: rather, try to maintain an upright position with your upper body.
- ❏ If you are thrown forwards, try to bridge the reins across the horse's neck, as this can help support you whilst you regain your balance; it will also prevent the horse from snatching the reins away from you. In practice, however, few riders will be sufficiently organized, or have the presence of mind to do this.

Bolting

Almost every rider will have had some experience of being 'carted' by a horse at some time, even if only for a short distance. If a horse tries to run away with his rider it is generally due to pain or fear; given the option, horses will almost always try to escape at speed from anything they perceive as threatening. It can also happen when they find themselves in an exciting situation, such as cantering or galloping in a group.

What To Do

- ❏ Keep your head and body upright or slightly behind the vertical.
- ❏ Keep both heels deep, and the lower legs pushed slightly forward.
- ❏ Take a strong grip on the reins, bracing your weaker hand against the top of the withers. This will help prevent you from being jerked forward out of the saddle and will counterbalance the effect of the other rein so you do not pull the horse over.
- ❏ Take very sharp, rapid jerks on the other rein.
- ❏ If you have a lot of space, try turning the horse's head slightly if you can, so as to bring it on to a large circle. This will have the effect of starting to slow its speed; as this happens, decrease the circle size until you have regained control.

What Not To Do

- ❏ Try to jump off – this can be more dangerous, as well as difficult to do, than staying put.
- ❏ Head the horse towards walls or fences. He may attempt to jump them, or may run head-first into them.
- ❏ Head into an expanse of water; it will slow him very effectively, but the speed at which he enters, combined with the drag of the water against his legs, is very likely to cause him to fall, and you could be trapped underneath.
- ❏ Turn the horse sharply unless you have to, as it will unbalance him and he is likely to fall.
- ❏ Chase after someone who is either having difficulty maintaining control, or has already lost it. Follow on at a slow and steady pace so you do not make the situation worse.

Napping

A horse that naps will come to a standstill and refuse to move any further; if urged forwards more strongly by the rider it may resort to rearing, attempting to spin round and head off in a different direction, cow-kicking, bucking on the spot, or running backwards.

Note that it is possible that a horse is not in fact being nappy at all, but is suffering the onset of muscle disorders: it is up to the rider to interpret the signs correctly.

The reasons why a horse becomes nappy may be many and varied, and include lack of confidence, fear of an object ahead, fatigue, pain or disobedience. Tact as well as firmness may be needed.

> ### See also
> ❏ Rearing, page 149
> ❏ Bucking, page 149
> ❏ Running Backwards, below
> ❏ Azoturia, page 64

What To Do

❏ Take care not to pull backwards on the reins as this will make the problem worse. Give the horse time to assess the situation ahead, and then ask it to move forward again.

❏ If it still remains glued to the spot, use both reins to shift the shoulders in a slightly sideways direction and then ask it to walk on once more. Take care that it does not seize the opportunity to whip round completely and set off at speed in the opposite direction.

❏ If you are riding in company, ask someone to give you a lead with their horse. If you are on your own, and feel you will have sufficient control from the ground, dismount and try leading the horse forward until you are past the problem area.

❏ If the horse still refuses to go forward, or continues to nap, you may have no other option but to return home either by a different route or by retracing your steps.

❏ If it is a persistent habit it is one that is best analysed, and the problem addressed by seeking expert professional help.

Running Backwards

This is an extreme form of napping, and it can be frightening and dangerous since the horse may reverse, often at speed, into something that may cause injury, or worse still, if on the road, into the path of traffic. There is also a possibility that as the horse moves backwards, so much weight is transferred over the quarters that it will find it easy to rear.

There are certain things you can do to try and regain control – and also things that you should try to avoid doing.

What To Do

- ❑ Try to avoid leaning forwards, as this will make it easier for the horse to run backwards.
- ❑ Take care not to have a restrictive rein contact, as this will further inhibit forward movement. Do not apply stronger leg aids or use a whip to try to enforce forward movement; it is more likely to make the horse even more bolshy.
- ❑ If you have sufficient space and it is safe to do so, circle the horse, although not so tightly that it rears or loses its balance and falls. This may enable you to regain control of its movement and to send it forwards.
- ❑ If the situation is one where there are too many potential hazards in the immediate environment; if you are unable to restore forward movement; if the horse is likely to rear; or if you feel that persisting may lead to you getting hurt – dismount immediately and lead the horse home. It is then most important that you seek expert advice.

Shying

A horse may shy when confronted by an object it perceives as threatening or frightening, or when startled by a sudden, unexpected movement. Some horses are more easily spooked than others, and cold, windy days and over-freshness are likely to exacerbate such behaviour.

Windy weather will also increase the likelihood of bags and other rubbish being blown around, so if your horse is easily spooked by such things, on a blustery day it may be advisable to exercise him by lungeing him, or riding him in an enclosed area, rather than hacking out.

Sometimes you will receive some advance warning, but more often than not the horse will react suddenly and abruptly, moving quickly away from the frightening object; and if you are on the roads, the risk of the horse stepping sideways into the path of passing traffic can be high, and could be dangerous.

What To Do

- ❑ Try to be alert at all times; however, do not make matters worse by becoming tense, as this will only cause the horse to be even more wary and on edge. The best policy is to ride forward calmly and confidently.
- ❑ If the horse starts to spook at something, do not pull his head towards it; rather, bend his head and neck away from the object, and use plenty of leg on the side he is flexed to. If he is familiar with shoulder-in, use this movement to enable you to ride safely past.
- ❑ If you are on the roads, ask your hacking companion to stop the traffic for you whilst you move to a safe area; wait until the road is clear before moving past the hazard. Remember to thank those who are patient and courteous.

3 First Aid For People

In this section

The First Aid Kit

Many horse owners keep at least a basic first aid kit for their horses, but rarely seem to feel it necessary to take the trouble to do the same for themselves. If you are fortunate you may never have to use it for more than the occasional sticking plaster, but if an accident does occur you could well have cause to be grateful that it's there!

A first aid kit can either be bought complete, or individual items can be purchased separately and placed in a suitable, sturdy and watertight box. This box should be:

❏ clearly labelled;
❏ quickly accessible: make sure everyone knows its location;
❏ checked regularly, and any contents replaced as necessary;
❏ kept in a cool, dry place.

POCKET FIRST AID KIT

As well as a first aid kit kept on the yard premises, also equip yourself with a small, pocket first aid kit for when you are out riding; good saddlers and chemists stock these in neat packs that can be slipped into a bumbag or attached to a D ring on your horse's saddle.

BASIC KIT

20 adhesive dressings (sticking plasters) of assorted sizes

10 sterile dressings: 6 medium-sized, 2 large, 2 extra-large

2 sterile eye pads

6 triangular bandages

a roll of cotton wool

6 safety pins in various sizes

2 pairs of disposable latex gloves

COMPREHENSIVE KIT – as Basic Kit plus:

a pair of blunt-ended scissors

a pair of blunt-ended tweezers

2 crêpe bandages

roll of microporous tape

plastic face shield (used when giving artificial ventilation)

non-alcoholic wound-cleansing wipes

gauze pads

blanket (don't rely on a horse rug)

Assessing the Situation/Casualty

If you are the first person on the scene of an accident it is important to assess the situation quickly, and prioritize the actions you take:

1 Make the area safe to protect both the casualty and others from further danger – for example, stopping traffic and catching loose horses if it is a road accident. Delegate tasks to others where possible.

2 Give emergency first aid; deal with the most serious conditions first.

3 Summon the emergency services if required. If a casualty is unconscious, unable to rise, dizzy, an unusual colour, having difficulties, or is in serious pain, call an ambulance immediately.

4 Remain with the casualty until help arrives. Report your observations to those taking over from you.

When going to the assistance of a casualty you first need to assess the extent of their injuries, and whether there are any life-threatening conditions. First of all check for consciousness: speak to them, shake them gently by the shoulders (gently in case head, neck or spinal injuries are present), pinch a bare area of skin. If there is no response, shout for help. Your immediate priorities are to:

- open the airway;
- maintain breathing;
- maintain circulation;
- obtain medical help urgently.

LEVEL OF CONSCIOUSNESS

As well as observing and recording breathing and circulation every 10 minutes whilst you are with a casualty, monitor their level of consciousness. Check times with your watch, and note any changes so you can report these to the attending paramedic. Is the casualty:

- completely aware;
- a bit groggy and confused;
- not properly aware of what's going on;
- showing no reaction at all to any stimuli, including shouting, shaking and pain?

DEALING WITH A CASUALTY

Above all, remember the golden rule 'Do no harm'.

DO NOT:

- Remove the riding hat.
- Offer food, liquids or cigarettes.
- Place yourself in danger.
- Attempt too much alone.
- Allow home anyone who has been unconscious, has suspected concussion (see Falling Off, page 139) or has had breathing difficulties: stay with the until medical help arrives.

DO:

- Remain calm.
- Alert the emergency services as quickly as possible.
- Prioritize – remember the ABC of first aid.
- Enlist help where possible.
- Reassure a conscious casualty.
- Avoid direct contact with body fluids where possible to avoid cross infection – wear protective gloves.
- Use common sense.

The ABC of First Aid

When dealing with a casualty, always remember the **ABC** of first aid:
Approach • **A**ssess • **A**irway • **B**reathing • **C**irculation

AIRWAY **Maintaining the airway is** always a priority.

Open the airway by placing two fingers under the chin and your other hand on the forehead, and tilting the head back. In this position the tongue is lifted from the back of the throat so that it doesn't block the air passage.

If you think there may be neck injuries, open the airway by kneeling at the head of the casualty with your knees on either side to keep it still. Placing a hand on each side of the head, position your fingers under the angle of the jaw, and gently lift it to open the airway.

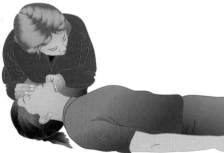

BREATHING **Check if the casualty is breathing** by putting your cheek close by the nose and mouth. Look along the line of the chest to see if it is rising and falling, listen for the sound of breathing, and feel for breath on your cheek. Carry out these checks for up to 10 seconds.

If breathing is present place the casualty in the recovery position (see Recovery Position, page 157).

If breathing is absent give artificial ventilation (see Artificial Ventilation page 158).

CIRCULATION **Check whether the heart is beating** by feeling the pulse; the easiest place to find this is the carotid pulse located in the hollow of the neck between the windpipe and the large neck muscle. Check the pulse for up to 10 seconds.

If a pulse is present but not respiration, continue with artificial ventilation.

If there is no pulse, start cardio-pulmonary resuscitation (CPR) (see Cardio-Pulmonary Resuscitation, page 159).

Check for bleeding, severe blood loss reduces the flow to vital organs and can result in severe shock. Control serious bleeding as soon as breathing and circulation is established.

The Recovery Position

A casualty who is unconscious but still breathing should be moved into the recovery position. This will help keep the airway open, it enables them to breathe easily, and ensures that if vomiting occurs it will drain out of the mouth and won't be inhaled or cause choking. The flexed limbs will keep the body propped securely, so that if forced to leave to get help, the casualty can be left safely in this position.

❶ Kneel beside the casualty.
Check for, and remove, any bulky items from the pockets.
Open the airway (see ABC of First Aid, page 156).
Straighten the legs and place the arm closest to you at right angles to the casualty's body as though they were waving to someone.

❷ Take the hand of the arm furthest away from you and place it palm facing outwards against the casualty's cheek, and hold it there.
With your other hand, draw up the knee of the casualty which is furthest from you, keeping the foot flat on the ground.

❸ Still keeping the casualty's hand pressed against their cheek, pull smoothly on the leg just above the knee to roll them towards you and on to their side.

❹ Tilt the head back slightly to ensure the airway remains open. Adjust the position of the hand beneath the cheek if necessary, and the upper leg so that the knee and hip are both bent at right angles.
Cover the casualty with a jacket, rug or blanket for warmth. Shock can cause a drop in body temperature even on warm days.

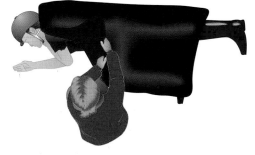

Artificial Ventilation

If breathing has stopped, you will have to breathe for the casualty to ensure that the body cells – especially those of the brain – continue to receive oxygen. The air that you breathe out contains around 16 per cent oxygen, and can save life if blown into the casualty's lungs; this procedure is called artificial ventilation.

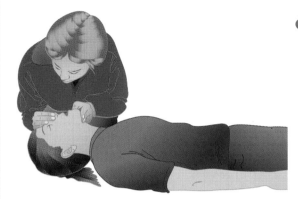

❶ **Open the airway** by tilting the casualty's head back by using two fingers under the chin and the other hand on the forehead. Remove any obvious obstruction, such as mud, or broken or displaced dentures, by using two fingers to gently scoop sideways in the mouth. If you have a plastic face shield place it over the casualty's mouth.
Pinch the casualty's nose between forefinger and thumb to close it.

❷ **Take** a full breath and place your lips over the casualty's mouth, making a good seal around it.
Blow into the casualty's mouth until you see the chest rise. It should take about two seconds for a full inflation.

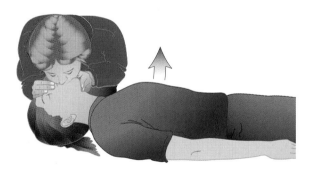

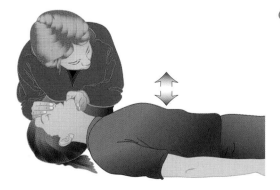

❸ **Keeping the nose pinched** between finger and thumb, remove your lips from the casualty's mouth and allow the chest to fall fully. This will take around four seconds to happen.
Give another breath, then check for signs of circulation.
If circulation is present, continue with ventilations and check the pulse again after every ten breaths you give. If the casualty begins to breathe again unaided, place in the recovery position.
If circulation is absent, begin cardio-pulmonary resuscitation (CPR) immediately.

Cardio-Pulmonary Resuscitation

If you cannot find a pulse, it means that the heart has stopped beating, and you will need to provide circulation artificially by giving chest compressions, accompanied by artificial ventilation. This procedure is called cardio-pulmonary resuscitation (CPR). Although unlikely to restart the heart, it ensures that oxygenated blood continues to reach the brain, buying time until help arrives.

If someone else is with you, delegate them to call for emergency medical services immediately. If you are on your own with the casualty, and the condition is due to injury or drowning, give resuscitation for one minute and then call for an ambulance. In any other circumstance, call an ambulance first and then begin resuscitation.

❶ **Kneel** beside the casualty.
Locate the lowermost rib on one side with the first two fingers of the hand, then slide them along the rib to where it meets the bottom of the breastbone.

❷ **Place** the heel of your other hand on top of the breastbone and then slide it downwards until the edge of the hand touches the forefinger of the first hand.
Put the heel of your first hand on top of the second and interlock the fingers together.

❸ **Lean forward** over the casualty, keeping your arms straight, and press downwards, depressing the breastbone about 4–5cm (1½–2in).
Release the pressure, but without moving the hands from their position.

❹ **Compress** the chest in this way 15 times, aiming to give around 100 compressions per minute. Then give two breaths of artificial ventilation.
Continue to alternate the sequence of 15 chest compressions with two breaths of air until help arrives.

Shock

Some injuries may cause a casualty to go into shock and if not treated this can prove fatal. Signs to be alert for include:

- initially rapid pulse becoming weak and thready as shock develops;
- paleness;
- dizziness;
- nausea and possibly vomiting;
- rapid, shallow breathing;
- sweating, and cold, clammy skin.

Treat any obvious cause of shock such as external bleeding.
Lie the casualty on a blanket, rug or coat to insulate them from the cold coming up from the ground.
Raise the legs to improve the blood supply to important internal organs. Be careful if fractures are suspected.

Keep the casualty warm by covering with jackets, or blankets.
Call for an ambulance.
Monitor and record breathing, circulation and level of response. Be prepared to resuscitate if necessary.

Fractures

Call for an ambulance.
Stem bleeding in the case of open fractures (where the skin has been broken by the underlying bone). Do not press down directly on any protruding bone ends (see Bleeding, opposite).
Gently steady and support the injured limb with a hand placed above and below the area. In the case of an arm injury, the casualty may prefer to do this themselves.
Treat for shock (see Shock, above).

Crush Injuries

Crush injuries to fingers and toes are not uncommon around horses; for example, feet get trodden on and fingers get trapped in stiff stable-door bolts or gates.

If the fingers are crushed and it is possible to do so, gently remove any jewellery before the area starts to swell.
Elevate the injured area.
Wrap soft padding around the injured area.
Arrange for the casualty to be taken to hospital.

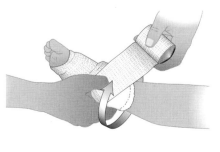

Bleeding

If an injury is bleeding, wear disposable gloves to help prevent the risk of cross-infection before dealing with the wound. If someone is with you and bleeding is severe, send them to call for an ambulance whilst you give emergency first aid. If you are on your own, follow steps 1–4 below, and then alert the emergency medical services.

❶ **Get the casualty to sit or lie down on the ground;** this helps reduce the blood flow to the site of the injury, and if they become faint or dizzy they will not sustain further injury if already at ground level.
Locate the source of the wound; it may sometimes be necessary to remove or cut clothing to reach it.
Stem bleeding by applying direct pressure to the wound with a clean pad.

❷ **Secure** the pad with a bandage.

❸ **If an object is embedded** in the wound do not attempt to remove it; apply firm pressure to a pad on each side of it. Build up the pads until they are high enough to bandage over the top without placing pressure on the object.
Raise and support the injured limb if possible above the level of the casualty's heart.
Check the colour of the skin beyond the bandage to ensure that the circulation is not being cut off whilst waiting for help to arrive.
If blood seeps through the bandage, apply further dressings on top..

❹ **If it is impossible** to apply direct pressure to a wound site you can use 'indirect pressure' instead. This is done by applying pressure with your fingers to a pressure point above the bleeding artery where the main vessel runs close to a bone.
Do not apply pressure in this way for more than ten minutes.
Never put on a tourniquet as this may make bleeding worse and can result in tissue damage.

Suspected Neck or Spinal Injury

If the casualty is conscious, you can ask if they can move their fingers and toes; if they cannot, or feel numb or tingling, assume that there may be a neck or spinal injury.

❶ **Move the casualty as little as possible** and only if it is absolutely necessary.
Ask other people, or use rolled clothing, blankets or rugs to help support the body on each side.

❷ **Kneel at the casualty's head** and place a hand to either side, over the ears to steady and support it.
Monitor continuously until help arrives in case the casualty loses consciousness, breathing or circulation

Unconscious Casualty

If the casualty is unconscious, check the breathing and circulation, and remember that resuscitation or maintaining an open airway should take priority over any possible risk of making a spinal injury worse.

❶ **Open the airway** (see page 156).

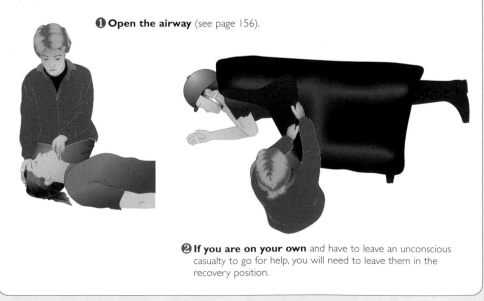

❷ **If you are on your own** and have to leave an unconscious casualty to go for help, you will need to leave them in the recovery position.

4 Accident Prevention

In this section

Security

Whilst it is impossible to make a yard 100 per cent secure, there are many measures you can take to make it a less easy or obvious target. Remember that anything you can do that will slow a thief down, will act as a deterrent.

❶ Security mark your horse and tack

Ways of doing this include microchipping, tattooing, hoof marking and freezebranding (see p.98); the latter is the most obviously visible, as well as being a permanent form of marking, and has proved to be very effective. Select a reputable company that operates a twenty-four-hour emergency service and maintains a national database. Find out what assistance is offered in the event of theft, too, such as rewards, liaising with the police, and notifying ports, slaughterhouses and auctions.

Display signs in prominent places around the yard and on field gates advertising the fact that horses and saddlery are security marked; as well as being a good deterrent, it avoids the problem of horses later being turned loose when marks are discovered.

in the search for your horse if he is stolen, as well as providing a positive ID that he is yours.

❸ Padlock yard and field gates

Use a heavy duty chain and lock; secure the hinge as well as the latch sides. **Do not padlock your horse into his stable, in case of fire.**

❹ Install floodlights and a burglar alarm

The floodlights will be activated by a motion sensor, and you may be able to link it to the alarm. If feasible, a CCTV system could also be installed. Clearly display a poster advertising the presence of an alarm system.

❷ Keep an identity pack

Keep a folder (at your home, not the yard) containing a complete description chart of your horse, with details of distinguishing marks. Include recent photographs taken from front and back, as well as both sides; this can assist

KEEP A GUARD DOG

A guard dog can also be a good deterrent: hang up a sign in a prominent position advertising the fact.

⑤Never leave keys hidden anywhere

⑥Install an alarm in the tackroom
Also, use some kind of permanent marking system on saddlery and rugs. Try to keep as much of it as possible at home, rather than at the yard. Devices that lock saddles to racks can also be used (below).

Tackrooms should have limited entry points, ideally through one door only, and this should be set in a solid frame. If there are any windows, they should be as high as possible and with security bars set inside; locks should be good ones – a simple padlock is not enough. Check that the roof is not a weak point, either. Do not put up signs advertising its location.

❼Fit a security system to vehicles
Secure lorries, trailers and towing vehicles. At shows, store saddlery in a secure trunk when not in use, and always leave your vehicle locked.

⑧Record details of suspicious vehicles
Make a note of any unusual vehicles you see near the yard. Ask neighbours to do the same, and to notify you of any strangers or suspicious activity they may notice.

Be suspicious of any strangers who approach you or visit the yard, and engage you in seemingly innocent conversation about any of the horses: do not provide any information about security systems.

⑨Vary the times you visit your horse
This will make it more difficult for a thief to judge times when the yard will be deserted.

⑩Make use of local resources
Ask your local Crime Prevention Officer to visit the yard. He will be able to comment on your current security arrangements, and suggest any improvements that could be made.

Find out if you have a Horsewatch group in your area – ask local riding clubs or equine welfare organizations for details, or look on the Internet for information.

DON'T INVALIDATE YOUR INSURANCE

Very often it is not just the horses, but all the other possessions kept at the yard, such as saddlery, rugs, horseboxes and trailers that are targets for thieves.

In a robbery that took place at a livery yard one winter, the thieves not only stole all the saddlery from the tackroom, but even took the rugs from the horses' backs — both those in the stables and those out in the field. Furthermore, many owners were horrified to find that their insurance companies refused to pay out for replacement saddlery due to the fact that the security arrangements for the tackroom did not fulfil the terms of the policy.

Fire Prevention and Yard Safety

A stable yard can be a potential death trap if a fire breaks out, so it is vital that sensible preventive measures are maintained at all times:

❶ Enforce a strict 'No Smoking' policy within the stable yard and in its immediate environs.

❷ Security measures should be taken to deter possible arson attacks (see Theft, page 111)

❸ Take extra care with all things electrical in the stable yard
- All electrical cables should be maintained in good order and protected with waterproof and rodent-proof covers.
- Any external electrical sockets should have waterproof covers; all light switches should also be waterproof, and located where they cannot be reached by the horse.
- Electrical fittings and appliances should be regularly checked by a qualified electrician.
- Light fittings in stables should be set high in the ceiling, using low-watt light bulbs with protective covers.
- Clippers, heaters and other electrical appliances should be unplugged when not in use.
- Rugs and other items of clothing should not be left on top of, or near heaters.

❹ Combustible materials should be treated carefully
Materials such as petrol, diesel or paint should be kept to a minimum, safely stored, and situated as far away from stabling as possible.

In the Event of a Fire

Certain measures should also be in place in case a fire does occur. Fire notices and equipment should be clearly displayed and easily accessible.

❶ Make sure an appropriate number of fire bells and notices are in place
These should be placed around the yard and ancillary buildings.

❷ Install smoke detectors in stables and barns
These should be checked monthly; also, vacuum and wipe the casings and slots regularly to prevent accumulations of dust and cobwebs from blocking the smoke sensor chamber. If they are mains-connected, rather than battery-operated alarms, disconnect them before cleaning.

❸ Ensure there is an adequate number of fire buckets and extinguishers
Fire extinguishers should be regularly serviced and of an appropriate type; your fire officer will be able to advise you on this. Hoses should be in good condition and sufficiently long.

❹ Yard gates should be wide enough to accommodate fire appliances

---

FIRE NOTICES

Fire notices should contain the following information:
- The sequence of actions to be taken in the event of a fire.
- Location of the fire bell.
- The location of the nearest telephone, the number to ring, and what information to give the fire services.
- Assembly points, and the paddocks to be used should horses need to be evacuated.
- Location of fire extinguishers, buckets and hoses.
- Location of first-aid facilities.

⑤ Keep exits and entrances clear of obstructions at all times

⑥ Keep door bolts and latches well maintained

They should be easy to open and shut, but not loose!

⑦ Keep a headcollar and leadrope hanging outside each horse's stable

⑧ Ask your local fire officer to check over your arrangements

He can offer advice on precautions and equipment.

Yard Safety

Even if a yard is not as smart as it might be, it can still be a safe environment. It is easy to become so used to your surroundings that you stop noticing them properly. Take a fresh look at them by spending half an hour walking around and jotting down all those things that could be a hazard to you or your horse:

❶ Pay attention to the state of the yard surface

Yard surfaces should be kept swept, and not be uneven or badly potholed; where drain covers are present, these should be strong enough to support a horse's weight.

Surfaces should be gritted during icy weather.

❷ Do not allow yard equipment to become hazards

Yard tools, wheelbarrows and mucking out implements should be stored safely in a suitable area, and not left outside the stable doors. Pitchforks should be hung up with the prongs facing inwards towards the walls.

Bales of bedding, skeps, saddlery and grooming kit should not be left lying around the yard where they might be tripped over.

❸ Muck heaps and barns should be situated well away from stabling

This reduces the risk of fire spreading to them.

❹ Stables and doorways should be of suitable design and dimensions

They should be appropriate for the horses kept in them, and maintained in good repair.

❺ Cars should be parked sensibly

Keep them away from horses and hay/straw stacks, and not obstructing access points.

❻ Dogs and children should be kept under control at all times

❼ Make sure fencing is suitable for horses, and kept well maintained

❽ Dispose of rubbish appropriately

❾ Wormers and medications should be stored safely and securely, especially if there are children around

❿ Keep feed-room doors closed

Protective Clothing for Riders

When you book your first lessons at a riding school, you are usually advised what to wear for both your comfort and safety; however, once you progress to keeping your own horse, these recommendations are unfortunately all too often disregarded. Wearing the correct clothes for riding is not just a matter of tradition or presenting a smart appearance: they are specifically designed for comfort, practicality and – just as important – protection, too.

The three main areas of concern are headgear, footwear and body protectors.

Headgear

Wearing a hard hat is vital for all mounted activities (and some dismounted ones, too) as head injuries can be grave, even fatal. Although a hard hat may not be able to prevent serious injury in all circumstances, there is no doubt that many lives have been saved by wearing one. Even if you do not hit your head directly during a fall, remember that a glancing blow from a hoof or even a low-hanging tree branch can just as effectively crack your skull.

In the UK it is a legal requirement that children aged fourteen years or younger wear correctly secured, protective headgear, that meets current approved safety standards, whilst riding on the road.

❶ **What to watch when buying a hat**
• **Go to a shop with staff trained in fitting them** to ensure that you get the right size, and that you are shown how to check and correctly secure the harness yourself. Even if you have owned a hat before and think you know your size, a retailer who is doing his job properly will still measure you up. A surprisingly large number of riders are sure their hat fits, but are actually wearing the wrong size.

• **Do not mistake firmness of fit for tightness,** or you could end up with a hat that is too large. Although a well fitting hat should not cause severe discomfort, it does need to be a snug fit. Be prepared to try several different makes until you find one that best matches your head shape.

• **Do not place the hat on the back of your head first,** as it will end up sitting too far back; put it on your forehead first and rock it back into position so that it sits squarely on the head.

• **Next adjust the harness; first the chinstrap, and then the rear fastenings according to the manufacturer's instructions.** Rear fastenings should sit comfortably at the base of the

skull. The harness needs to be secure, so that it isn't possible to remove the hat once fastened, but not to the point of choking you. Remember that although it will prevent the hat tipping forwards or coming off, the harness will not make a hat fit correctly if the size is wrong.

• **Check that it meets with current safety standards.** Hat safety is of the utmost importance, so never buy a secondhand hat, because you simply don't know its history. Novice riders are usually able to hire a hat from riding centres when initially starting out, but once the decision has been made to continue riding on a regular basis, this should be the first, and is certainly the most important, item of riding clothes to invest in.

❷ **Discard or replace a damaged hat with a new one**

If you have a fall and hit your head, or drop your hat on to a hard surface, even though there may be no visible sign of damage, the level of protection offered may be greatly reduced by the impact. This may seem like an expensive policy, but it is far easier and less costly to replace a hat than a head!

❸ **Secure your harness at all times**

There is little point in wearing a hard hat if the retaining harness is not secured: do not leave it unfastened.

❹ **Look after your hat**

Only use cleaning methods recommended by the manufacturer; and don't leave your hat in hot places, because extreme heat, such as in the back window of the car on a hot day, can distort it.

Footwear

❶ **Make sure that your footwear will not become wedged in or slip through the irons**

Wedge heels, sandals and wellington boots (above) are not suitable footwear for riding. Neither are trainers, except those made by equestrian manufacturers and designed specifically for riding in. Suitable footwear should not have heavily ridged soles, but should have a defined heel (below) of not less than ½in (1.25cm), and not more than 1in (2.5cm).

❷ **Use protective footwear when handling horses**

Even a small pony standing on your toes can be an agonizing, and sometimes bone-breaking, experience. Steel toecaps have had a bad press in the past due to substandard products appearing on the market; however, they are nowadays much improved – although you should make sure that such boots (and not just the packaging) are CE marked, and also carry a safety standard mark.

Protective Clothing for Riders

Body Protectors

At one time you would only ever see jump jockeys and horse trials' riders wearing body protectors, and even then it was on an entirely voluntary basis. Nowadays, however, their design has become far more sophisticated and effective, to the extent that they are frequently worn for choice by leisure riders, as well as being compulsory in certain competitive disciplines.

Falling off inevitably carries a risk of being trodden on or kicked, as well as of injuries incurred through hitting the ground or contacting a tree or a jump, for example, and a body protector can help to cushion the blow. The best will offer some protection to vital organs, can prevent minor bruising, reduce significant soft tissue injuries to the level of bruising, and prevent a limited number of rib fractures. What they won't do is prevent injuries involving severe torsion, flexion, extension, or crushing of the body.

❶ Go to a reputable retailer

As when buying a hard hat, go to a retailer with staff who are trained in fitting, and who will be able to give you advice on how to put it on and adjust it correctly yourself. A retailer should not sell you a body protector without measuring you up first to ensure you are given the correct size.

❷ Make sure you are measured

You will need to be measured from the waist, up over the shoulder and down the back to the base of the spine, as well as around the chest and waist.

❸ Make the necessary adjustments to achieve a close fit

Having obtained the appropriate size, it will then need to be adjusted to give a close fit. A design that will mould to the shape of your body over a period of time will be better than one that is very stiff and flat-fronted, making your chest feel compressed, and with a propensity to ride up, too. Body heat may also affect the fit, so wait a few minutes before making final adjustments.

Look out for the following:

- The body protector should have a secure and reasonably firm fit to prevent it moving around, and to ensure that it stays in place in the event of a fall.

- It should not catch on the saddle when the wearer is riding.

- It should cover the whole circumference of the torso.

- The back should reach the prominent bone at the base of the neck.

- At the front the bottom edge should be not less than 25mm below the last rib and should reach the level of the pelvis.

- The holes for the arms should be circular and as small as possible.

- It should be comfortable to wear in all riding positions and not impede flexibility or hamper movement.

UK STANDARDS

In the UK there are three standards of body protector: Class 1 offers the lowest level of protection, Class 2 the minimum recommended level for normal riding, and Class 3 the highest level.

A body protector that is too large will offer reduced protection; therefore when purchasing for children, do not buy one to be 'grown into'.

Clothing and Safety

Here are some other considerations concerning clothing, in its relation to safety:

❶ Gloves will protect the hands

When riding or leading, gloves will protect the hands from blisters and friction burns. Those with rubber pimples on the palms will also give a better grip.

❷ Use spurs with discretion

Do not wear spurs when riding an unknown horse for the first time. Also remove them when handling any horse: it is very easy for the shanks to become entangled if you step backwards or sideways, which can trip you up.

❸ If you wear a jacket, do it up

Do not leave it open and flapping, which may spook your horse. Never attempt to remove a jacket whilst mounted, for the same reason.

❹ If you wear spectacles: plastic lenses are safer than glass ones

Also, rigid frames can break in the event of a fall and cut your face, so it is sensible to invest in a pair with flexible frames.

❺ Always protect your arms

If the weather is hot, wear a light shirt, but not a singlet, a sleeveless T-shirt – or less! Even lightweight fabric sleeves will give some protection against scrapes and grazes in the event of a fall.

❻ Leave your jewellery at home

Earrings, bracelets, necklaces, rings and body piercings can all cause injuries while handling horses, as well as during riding activities.

❼ Wear the correct gear when handling horses

Wear a hard hat, gloves and sturdy footwear when handling horses as well as during riding activities. The results of a survey conducted by an equestrian insurance company revealed that the largest proportion of equine-related injuries to humans actually occur in the stables or while leading.

❽ When buying new protective clothing check with official bodies as to the latest standards

Standards are subject to change: if you are planning to compete, look through the official rule books, or contact the governing body of the sport to ensure that your garments meet their guidelines; different disciplines may require differing levels of protection.

CLOTHING AND COMFORT

Comfort whilst riding also contributes to safety: if clothing rubs or irritates, a good riding position will often be compromised, and the rider's attention distracted from what the horse is doing.

- Jodhpurs perform ideally because they allow free movement, whilst seams are strategically positioned and designed so as not to cause chafing in crucial parts of the anatomy!
- Underwear is also worthy of mention at this point, too. Men are likely to be more comfortable in close-fitting Y-front type underpants rather than boxers; ladies should avoid lace-edged garments or thongs, and whilst a well-fitting bra offering good support can also make life more comfortable, underwired ones should not be worn as the wires can work loose and penetrate an armpit.

Protective Equipment for Horses

Stable and Working Boots

Boots or bandages may be needed on certain occasions to protect your horse from injuries caused by knocks and bumps whilst he is working, or in the stable, or when travelling.

There is a huge variety of different types of boot available, offering protection to the limbs; if you aren't sure what to buy, ask your instructor or saddler for advice on the matter.

❶ Fitting boots

You should first check that they are the right size for your horse; if not, they will not offer maximum protection, and could interfere with your horse's action, causing discomfort or even becoming dislodged so they trip him up.

❷ Securing boots

They must be secured firmly enough to keep them in position, but not so tightly that they inhibit circulation or joint flexion.

❸ Linings

These should be kept scrupulously clean – if dirt and dried sweat are allowed to accumulate they can chafe the legs badly.

❹ Fastenings

Take care with fastenings: they should be positioned on the outside of the leg so they do not come undone as a result of interference from the opposite leg. Boots with velcro fastenings are quicker and easier to put on and take off than those with buckles and straps. However, the velcro does need to be clean to work efficiently, and it is a sensible precaution to tape these over for extra security.

Bandages

It is a matter of personal preference as to whether you use boots or bandages for leg protection during exercise or when travelling; for the majority of people, boots are quicker, easier and safer. Good bandaging is a skill that takes practice to acquire, and tremendous harm can be done if they are badly applied (see Bandaging, page 20).

❶ Bandages should be put on over a layer of padding

Use gamgee or padding such as Fybagee.

❷ Fastenings should be secured as high as possible on the bandage and towards the outside of the limb

Tapes should be kept flat, and tied in a flat knot – not a slipknot – that rests between bone and tendon. For extra security, either stitch in place or apply insulating tape over the top. Fastenings should only be as tight as the bandage itself.

PROTECTION WHEN EXERCISING

If riding one horse and leading another at exercise, make sure that both horses wear boots to protect their legs from each other should one or other shy, or start jumping about. It is also recommended that overreach or coronet boots are put on the front feet of the led horse and the hind feet of the ridden one to reduce the risk of tread injuries.

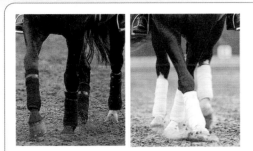

❸ Keep an eye on bandages that become wet during exercise

They may stretch and begin to slip. Remove them as soon as possible after work because they can shrink as they dry out, tightening on the leg.

Travelling Protection

For travel, and also when practising loading, the horse should be adequately protected against knocks and bumps should he slip or become unbalanced. He may also need to be rugged up if the weather is cold and/or wet.

❶ Make sure that the rug is fitted with either hindleg straps or a fillet string

This will prevent it being blown up over the horse's back and frightening him when he is outside the vehicle. (For the same reason a fillet string should also be attached to exercise sheets and rain sheets.)

❷ Use a poll guard, tail bandage, and a tail guard for additional protection

Many rugs have a D ring stitched into the top centre seam to which tail-guard tapes can be tied to keep it in place. If the tapes are tied to a roller or surcingle instead, make sure that pressure is not placed on the spine, and also use a breast-girth to prevent the roller slipping backwards.

❸ Use travelling boots or bandages

Boots are very quick and easy to put on compared to bandages, and modern designs incorporate knee and hock protection. However, they do need to be a good fit if they are to be safe. Wash new ones before use to loosen them up a bit, as they can be stiff initially, which makes it difficult to fit them securely.

If bandages are used instead of travelling boots, knee and hock boots should be worn. Make sure that you bring a bandage right down to cover the coronet area so as to protect it from treads; alternatively use overreach or coronet boots.

Hi-Visibility (Hi-Vis) Clothing

Hi-vis clothing will not actually protect either you or your horse in the event of a traffic-related accident – but it could help to ensure that it doesn't happen in the first place.

Not many riders are in the happy position of being able to avoid going out on the roads altogether; even in areas where off-road riding along bridleways and trails is available, reaching these tracks often entails having to negotiate at least a short stretch of public highway. With traffic on roads growing steadily busier these days, staying safe is therefore a high priority for most riders, and this aim can be partly achieved by ensuring that both you and your horse are as highly visible as possible. According to the British Horse Society (BHS), the excuse that is most often given by motorists in the UK who have collided with a horse is, 'I just didn't see it' – which really does bring home the importance of this point. It's not enough to wear light-coloured clothing: to really stand out, specialized hi-vis garments and accessories should be used.

Riding in Daylight Hours

In daylight hours, fluorescent clothing shows up best, and is available now not just in yellow, but also in orange, pink and lime green. A special pigment is used in the dyes, which is better able to absorb ultra-violet light, thereby helping to enhance the colour and make it more immediately vivid than any other colour, including white. According to the BHS, wearing fluorescent clothing enables a motorist to see you on average about three seconds more quickly; this means that a driver travelling at 50mph (80km/h) will have an extra 66m of braking distance, so although a few seconds may not seem like much time, in practice it could make all the difference between him hitting you, and being able to slow down sufficiently to pass by safely.

Riding in Dim Light Conditions

In dim light conditions, fluorescent clothing is rather less conspicuous and will just appear dull; in this case reflective clothing is more suitable because it will shine in car headlights and can reflect up to 3,000 times more light back to the driver than white clothing. The best garments are those with a combination of both fluorescent and reflective materials – check carefully for this at purchase.

Although riders are generally aware of the need to increase their visibility whilst hacking out on dull days during the winter months, not so many appreciate that they should adopt this policy all the year round, assuming that it will not be necessary during the long, bright days of summer. However, statistics collated by the BHS reveal that there is no difference in the accident rate between summer and winter, and that accidents occur at all times of the day, not just at dusk or in the early morning.

The majority of horses are bay, black or chestnut, colours that blend into the background during the summer (right) just as effectively as in the winter – and if

hi-vis garments are not worn, it is all too easy for a motorist not to spot you until it is too late. Bear in mind, too, that bright sunlight will often cause glare on the windscreen, making it hard for drivers to see a rider on the road ahead, as will deep shade beneath trees.

Essentials of What to Wear

❶ Hat cover or band
Especially useful when riding along twisty roads bordered by high hedges – it may be the first indication a driver will have that a rider is just ahead.

❷ Waistcoat or tabard
These will catch the attention of motorists approaching from either direction.

❸ Reflective leg bands
Use these on all four of your horse's legs; if you only have two, place them on the fore and hind legs closest to the centre of the road. Because they are constantly moving, they will quickly attract a driver's attention; also, their low position means they are picked up sooner by car headlights, making them very effective.

❹ Hi-vis exercise sheet and/or tailcover
This is your most vulnerable area, with statistics showing that 33 per cent of traffic accidents involve the horse being hit from behind.

❺ Hi-vis nose/browband and/or neckband
These get the attention of oncoming motorists.

Additional Accessories

As well as those mentioned above, other useful accessories well worth purchasing include:

❶ Gloves with fluorescent and reflective patches on the backs and reflective armbands
To draw attention to hand signals.

❷ Hi-vis covers for reins

❸ Clip-on lights

These lights can be obtained from cyclist shops, and can be constant or flashing. Highly visible and light-weight, they are ideal for attaching to saddlery, the horse's boots, and your own clothing as a back-up to hi-vis garments.

❹ Stirrup lights
Also available from most good saddlery shops: they should be attached with the white light facing towards the front, and the red light towards the rear.

'BE SEEN, BE SAFE'
Remember this apposite BHS slogan.
- Wear hi-vis clothing and accessories at all times of the day, irrespective of the season or weather conditions.
- Avoid taking your horse out on the roads in conditions of poor visibility – this includes driving rain, sleet and fog, as well as at dusk or dawn.
- Be aware that even on a bright winter's day the light can fade quickly, so when planning rides, ensure that you allow enough time to get home.
- Don't be deterred from using hi-vis clothing by the attitude of other riders, who may mock you for being excessively safety-conscious, or who simply feel that it's not 'cool' to wear it. Road safety is an issue that every responsible rider should take seriously.
- Even if you're only just going down the road, kit yourself up just as if you were going out for a longer ride – road accidents have happened within just yards of stepping out through the yard gates.

Saddlery

The saddlery your horse is ridden in can contribute to your safety, security, comfort and control; if inappropriate or poorly maintained, it can compromise all of these and instead make an accident more likely to happen. There are many good books on the use and selection of saddlery, and these are worth reading; but it is also important to consult an expert saddler.

Saddle

❶ The saddle should be suitable for the activity undertaken

For example, a dressage saddle is not designed for jumping.

❷ It is vital that the saddle fits both rider and horse correctly

The discomfort caused by an ill-fitting saddle can cause undesirable behaviour in the horse, and affect rider stability and general position. As there is more to saddle fitting than simply checking that the front arch clears the withers when the rider is mounted, it's worth the expense involved in engaging the services of a qualified saddle fitter. Most will be happy to visit your horse with a selection of different saddles for you to try out. Bear in mind that the stuffing in the panels can become compressed with use, and that your horse's shape can change with age, work, and also between summer and winter; therefore regular checks should be made to ensure that a good fit is maintained.

❸ Check the stirrup bars each time you ride

If a small catch (the thumbpiece) is present on the end of the stirrup bars, ensure this is pushed into the 'down' position so that it lies horizontally, in line with the bar. Should you fall off and a foot gets trapped in a stirrup, the leather will then be able to slide more easily off the stirrup bar.

❹ Check the quality and fit of the stirrup irons

For strength, the irons should be manufactured from high quality stainless steel. Should you lose a stirrup, the heavier type will move around less and be easier to locate again with a toe; adding rubber stirrup treads can also be helpful in making the stirrup iron less slippery, and thus easier to keep your feet in the correct place. The tread of the irons should be 1in (2.5cm) wider than the widest part of your boots, to avoid the risk of the feet becoming trapped; if they are too wide, the foot risks sliding right through.

All the buckles on stirrup leathers, girths and bridles should be of stainless steel for strength and safety.

Bridle

❶ The bridle should be suitable for the activity undertaken

A cross-country event is not the place to show off your lightweight, bootstrap show bridle.

❷ It is vital that the bridle fits the horse correctly

A seemingly minor detail such as a slightly tight browband, for example, can cause the headpiece to be pulled forward into the base of the ears. This will cause it to pinch, and can lead not just to soreness, but problems such as the horse becoming generally headshy, and tossing the head when ridden.

❸ The bit should be adjusted to fit correctly

The bit should be adjusted to the correct height in the mouth, and the mouthpiece itself should be of a suitable width and diameter for the conformation of the horse's mouth. In certain situations where a horse is inclined to become strong or excitable – for instance, when jumping – it may be advisable to use a bit that gives more control than the one normally used for quiet flatwork sessions at home.

❹ The reins should be sturdy enough for the activity they are used for

They should not be so wide that you have difficulty in holding them. Those with grips incorporated can help you keep control if they become slippery with rain or sweat. Rubber-covered reins should not be re-covered when the rubber eventually wears through, as it will be impossible to restitch exactly into the original holes, and this will cause weakness in the leather beneath. It is also important that reins are not so long that the rider's foot can become caught up in them.

Maintenance

❶ Buy only quality products
Avoid second-hand leather goods; although they may look and feel well cared for, the appearance can be deceptive. Previous neglect may mean that the leather is bone dry in the centre, and can snap without warning.

❷ Replace or repair items before they reach a critical state
❸ Clean your saddlery regularly
❹ Check tack frequently for signs of wear or damage

SAFETY CHECKS

- **Check your saddlery from both sides before mounting,** and particularly if someone else has tacked up for you.
- **Take all your saddlery apart at least once a week,** in order to clean and check thoroughly those areas that are difficult to access, such as where bridle cheekpieces and reins are attached to the bit.
- **When inspecting your tack check:**
  bit mouthpieces: no sharp edges/wear;
  buckle tongues: bent or worn short; `
  leather: worn areas that have become stretched, thin or distorted;
  hook studs: (used to attach bit to bridle and reins) not loose and wobbly;
  buckle holes: do not run into each other;
  stitching: is not weak; tug gently to test it;
  saddle panels: no areas of bagging or lumpiness in the saddle panels;
  stirrup bars: absolutely firm, with no movement in them.
- **All leatherwork should feel firm and greasy;** if it is blistered or wrinkled it may be weak and unsafe.
- **Saddle trees can break,** usually across the front arch or at the waist; and the tree can twist or become distorted. If you think there may be a problem, ask a saddler to check it for you.

Safe Hacking

Hacking out can be used as part of a fittening programme for your horse, as well as providing variety in his exercise regime; but for many riders, going out for a ride is simply an enjoyable and relaxing pastime. It can, however, be just as hazardous as any other equestrian activity if precautions are not observed.

❶ Equip yourself with the items listed in 'What to Take on a Ride' (see right)

❷ Always tell someone where you are going and when to expect you back

Try not to ride out unaccompanied: go out with at least one other person, and preferably with two others so that in the event of an emergency there will be plenty of help on the scene.

❸ Take care when crossing farmland

Avoid riding through fields where cattle or loose horses are grazing.

❹ Avoid cantering or galloping along every stretch of grass you encounter

If you always canter in the same spots, your horse will soon learn these, and anticipation may make him excitable and difficult to control.

❺ Try to plan circular routes

Doubling back on your tracks can encourage nappiness in some horses.

A FORTUNATE OUTCOME

After a prolonged spell of wet weather, on leaving work one evening in late autumn, Debbie was pleased to find that it had stopped raining, and on the spur of the moment decided to make the most of it and take her horse for a hack. Part of her route followed a track around some large fields, and this offered an ideal opportunity for a good gallop. The last thing she can remember doing before waking up in hospital was sending him on into a strong canter. Judging from the skid marks and the amount of mud covering one side of Monty – who fortunately remained by her – it appears that he slipped in a boggy area of ground, lost his balance and fell.

Debbie was discovered unconscious several hours later by a lady walking her dog, who was alerted by the sight of a riderless and unattended horse. Debbie recovered consciousness whilst in hospital, but the severe jarring which her brain had received left her partially paralysed, and it took many months of physiotherapy before she was once again able to walk without the aid of a stick. The route Debbie had taken was not often used at that time of year, and as she hadn't told anyone, or even left a note to say where she was going, it could have been days, rather than a matter of hours, before she was found.

In the event of a serious accident such as this, a delay of even minutes can make a vital difference, and Debbie was fortunate that the outcome was not worse.

❻Keep a sensible distance between each horse to avoid the risk of kicking

❼Be aware of conditions underfoot

- Remember that the surface of bridleways can deteriorate rapidly in wet weather, becoming boggy or treacherously slippery underfoot.

- Take local advice when riding in an area new to you, as to those parts best avoided, or hazards to watch out for.

- Don't go faster than a walk when riding along grass verges – they can conceal a multitude of hidden hazards such as rubbish, uneven going and overgrown drainage ditches.

❽Shorten your stirrups by 1–3 holes from their normal flatwork length
This will give you greater security, and make it easier to remain in a good balance when tackling gradients.

❾Do not go faster than your horse is fit enough to cope with. Do not ride in a sloppy fashion

❿Be considerate to other horses and riders you meet whilst out as well as those accompanying you

WHAT TO TAKE ON A RIDE

Even if you are only going for a short ride, equip yourself with this essential kit. Most of it can be fitted into either your jacket pockets in colder weather, or in a bumbag if it is warmer. Use the saddle Ds to attach things to, or buy a saddle cloth with pockets to put items in.

- **Pocket first-aid kit (see p154)**
- **Folding hoofpick**
- **Leadrope:** neatly coiled up and clipped to one of the front saddle D-rings.
- **Whistle:** to draw attention to your location; blowing a whistle is less tiring than shouting, and tends to carry better than your voice.
- **Mobile phone** (fully charged but turned off)
- **Phone card and/or change** for payphones
- **Length of baler twine**
- **Small notepad and safe writing implement** such as a piece of wax crayon
- **Neckstrap:** a stirrup leather in good repair doubles as a handy grab-strap to help you keep your balance, and as a 'spare' should one of your leathers break
- **Rider ID**: include your name, address, next of kin and their telephone number, and also the name and number of your GP and your vet. If you take any medication or have a history of problems such as allergy, diabetes or epilepsy, add this information. Slip the card into a pocket, not the lining of your hat.
- **Horse ID**: if you fall off, your horse may not hang around, so it is important that whoever finds him knows who to contact. Attach dog ID tags to a saddle D-ring and to the bridle. Include your name, your own or the yard telephone number, and also that of your vet. An engraved disc is more reliable than the screw-up capsule type, which can come apart.
- **Map and compass:** if you are planning a longer ride, or exploring an unfamiliar area.

Riding on the Roads

Horses were around long before the motor car, but this does not mean that riders have more rights than drivers: responsibility for road safety is a joint obligation. If you have no choice but to ride out along roads, observe the following precautions:

❶ Avoid using roads at peak hours

❷ Keep an eye out for potential hazards
Look out for potential problems ahead that might cause your horse to shy, such as dustbins and road bollards: try and pass such objects when there is a gap in passing traffic.

❸ Treat traffic with caution
• **If a large vehicle is approaching** which you think may alarm your horse, turn into a gateway or side road to allow it to pass at a safe distance.
• **Be careful when passing parked cars** as someone may be about to get out; dogs inside barking as you pass may also startle your horse.
• **Ride on the correct side of the road** moving with the flow of traffic; this also applies if you are leading a horse, but place yourself between him and the traffic.
• **Listen for the approach of traffic** from either direction, and look over your shoulder regularly to check for vehicles coming up behind you.
• **Thank motorists who slow down and who show consideration**

❹ Don't slop along; keep your horse moving forwards

❺ Do not ride out on roads known to be dangerous
Don't ride out after snow or ice, or when the light is failing, after dark, or when conditions are foggy

❻ Use a schoolmaster
Don't attempt to accustom an inexperienced horse to going out on the roads without the presence of a steady escort horse.

❼ Do not ride more than two abreast
Ride in single file where roads narrow, when approaching tight bends, or where visibility is otherwise poor, such as the approach to a humpbacked bridge.

❽ Be sensible when riding in a group
When riding out as part of a group, if you need to cross a road, do so together, and do not trickle across in ones and twos. If you go out in a group of more than eight riders, split into two smaller parties to make it easier and safer for vehicles to overtake you.

⑨ Give clear and accurate signals

Learn the correct hand signals to indicate your intentions when turning left or right, or if you require a motorist to slow down or stop.

⑩ Learn how to ride a roundabout (UK)

At roundabouts, stay to the left within the roundabout until reaching your exit, when you should signal left. Only signal right when approaching exits you do not intend to use.

RIDING AND ROAD SAFETY TIPS

In the UK, it is worth contacting the British Horse Society (BHS) to find out more about their Riding & Road Safety Tests. These tests aim to help educate riders, and also to minimize the risk to them when riding on the roads; they are currently taken by around 7,000 riders each year. Even if you do not take the test, you should certainly familiarize yourself with the appropriate sections of *The Highway Code*, and read the *BHS Riding and Road Craft Manual*.

Hand signals

Signalling that you intend to turn left

Signalling that you intend to turn right. Keep to the left of the road even when planning to turn right at a junction. Positioning your horse where he is sandwiched between lines of traffic with no escape route can be dangerous

Asking an approaching motorist to slow down by waving your arm up and down with the palm flat

Asking an approaching motorist to stop by raising your arm with the palm turned towards the driver. You may need to do this if you sense that your horse is about to act up in a potentially dangerous way or because you are aware of a car approaching in the opposite direction, which may be unseen by the first driver

Schooling Safely

Even if your main pleasure is hacking out, making time for a little regular schooling work will help to ensure that your horse remains supple, well balanced, obedient and responsive, making him a safer and more enjoyable ride. Although you can incorporate some schooling exercises into your hacking, you will find that working in a suitable area offers more scope. You may be fortunate and have access to an indoor school or outdoor arena with an all-weather surface, or be able to hire such facilities locally. Alternatively, in the summer you could use an area of grazing instead; if you do not actually own it, be sure to ask the landowner's permission.

When working in a field, there are certain precautions you should take:

❶ Choose an area of level, well drained ground

Trim back any rough, tussocky patches of grass which may cause your horse to trip.

❷ Make sure the area is well away from hazards

Do not ride in areas where other animals are grazing. Low, overhanging tree branches, barbed wire or electric fences are all potential problems.

❸ Take care when the ground is hard

Working on ground which is hard and dry during the summer months may cause jarring and concussion-related injuries.

❹ Be cautious when riding on wet grass

This can be very slippery, and riding in boggy conditions may also lead to injury. At such times it will be best to find somewhere else to work your horse, preferably a good all-weather surface.

However, even purpose-built riding surfaces can occasionally prove hazardous, and you should keep an eye out for potential problems:

❺ Watch out for membranes rising through the surface

❻ Avoid boggy patches due to uneven drainage or sprinkling

❼ Avoid poorly maintained surfaces

This will result in a hard-packed base with a loose covering of material on top.

When schooling, remember to:

❽ Warm up and cool down properly

Warm up properly in an active walk to reduce the risk of injury. Cool down at the end of a session, over a period of at least ten minutes.

❾ Keep your work varied

If you are not sure what to do with your horse, or if you run out of ideas quickly, invest in a few lessons with a good instructor.

❿ Finish on a good note and before your horse is feeling really tired

Working a tired horse not only invites the risk of injury, but also of misbehaviour. Praise and reward your horse after a good effort.

Jumping Safely

Most riders enjoy jumping, but it increases the potential for injury unless a few commonsense precautions are observed.

❶ Make sure that the ground conditions are suitable for jumping

If the going is deep or muddy following rain, your horse is at greater risk of strains and slipping. On the other hand, in dry weather the ground can rapidly harden and your horse's limbs will suffer from the effects of concussion.

❷ Always warm up on the flat first

Start with smaller fences and build up to larger ones. Be sure to approach fences from the correct side for the type of obstacle. When building combinations of fences, or grids for schooling purposes, set distances that are appropriate for your horse. Never try to catch him out, and do not ask him to jump higher or wider than he can cope with, or to constantly perform at the limit of his ability.

❸ Know when to end the session

Jumping demands a big athletic effort and can often be far more tiring than you realize. A horse that is tiring will be more likely to make a mistake – but remember that those with more excitable temperaments may not always show obvious signs of fatigue whilst actually jumping.

In particular beware of overdoing things at competitions: probably two show-jumping classes would be enough, or one cross-country class (depending on the length of the course).

❸ Take care in putting up fences at home

• **Use poles of a contrasting colour** to the surface you are riding on, so they do not merge into the background, becoming difficult for your horse to see.

• **Always use flat jump cups for planks, gates and hanging fillers; similarly, use shallow rather than deep jump cups for round poles,**

otherwise they may not be dislodged if knocked. This could result in a fall, and if the whole fence falls over there is a very real danger that the horse's legs may become entangled in it, further increasing the risk of serious injury.

• **Do not use any materials that could be hazardous** if your horse hits them: for example, legs may become trapped in tyres, and oil drums may roll and bring the horse down.

❹ Don't jump fences that have empty cups left on the wings

These can cause a wound if hit or fallen on.

❺ Don't leave jump cups or pins on the ground

They can cause a wound if trodden on or fallen on.

❻ Do not build fences with a false groundline

All elements of a fence beneath the top rail should either be in a direct vertical line below it, or drawn forward to the front of the approach side.

Horse and Rider Compatibility

Mismatches between horse and rider are often the reason behind many problem behaviours and accidents. If you ride at a riding school, the horse selected for you will probably be the most suitable in size, build, temperament and experience for your level of ability; and the same 'rules' should apply when you are considering purchasing, loaning or sharing a horse.

❶ Size does matter!

A horse that is too big or too small, too broad or too narrow for you can cause various rider problems, including those of stability, security and control. A tall horse is also more likely to create difficulties in stable management for a short owner/rider, when they can't reach to brush it or tack it up; and a leg-up or a mounting block is not always available when they want to get on!

❷ Weight-carrying ability is important

This can vary considerably between individual horses, not just according to height, but also conformation and age. A rider who is too heavy for the horse will cause it considerable discomfort, and this will lead to evasive behaviour as well as poor movement, which in turn can lead to problems such as stumbling or even falling.

❸ The horse's level of schooling must suit the rider

A novice horse and an equally novice rider do not make a good combination. Even if a rider is basically competent in their riding ability, a high level of experience and knowledge is also essential when riding a young horse.

❹ Horse and rider should be suited as regards temperament

The breeding and sex of the horse can sometimes, though not always, play a role in this. Thus highly strung animals will need a competent, sensitive, knowledgeable, calm and patient rider; whilst horses that are more laid back and placid in temperament will tend to be more forgiving of 'pilot errors', and will not be upset by the less experienced or less organized rider. A rider who is abrupt, nervous or inexperienced will soon get into difficulties with a 'hotter' horse.

❺ Horse and rider should be suited as regards ambition

Rider ambition can play a significant part in the rider/horse relationship, and many riders are guilty of wanting to attempt too much too soon, wishing to progress before either they or their horse is really ready for the next stage. Another scenario is that a talented competition horse may be too much for an inexperienced rider to cope with; whilst one that is less physically capable or lacks education may not be able to meet the demands of an over-ambitious rider.

❻ Take the advice of an expert

For those who intend buying a horse, taking one on loan, or having a part share in one, if you don't have a great deal of experience or knowledge in these matters, it would be advisable to take along someone who is more experienced when you go to see it. Preferably this will be your regular instructor, who is familiar with your riding ability, and is also more likely to be honest about the animal's suitability for you than a friend would be.

Handling Unknown Horses

You should always exercise care when handling and/or riding an unknown horse for the first time. You may be considering buying or loaning a horse; swapping horses with a friend can also be fun to try occasionally; and if you are a riding school client you are unlikely to be allocated the same animal every time you ride.

❶ Never be complacent

No matter what the owner/handler tells you.

❷ Spend time in advance with any horse you have been asked to look after

Become familiar with the horse and his usual routine. Find out about any quirks or behavioural traits, any precautions you should take, and ask for a written list containing details of feeding and contact numbers.

❸ Be correct in handling procedures

Even if the owner doesn't observe correct procedures *you* want to ensure that accidents do not occur. The horse may be less relaxed and confident when the owner isn't present. This applies when handling any horse that is strange to you; and if you have acquired a new horse, introduce new situations gradually.

❹ If you have to ride an unknown horse take proper precautions

• Don't mount up immediately, but introduce yourself to the horse from the ground first.

• Even if the horse has just been ridden, check that the saddlery is correctly fitted and adjusted, and that the girth is still tight enough. Take responsibility for your own safety: even if someone else insists on doing it for you, double check. For example, check the stirrup irons are going to be the right size for your feet.

• Adjust both stirrup leathers to approximately the length you will need so that should the horse be difficult once you are in the saddle you are not distracted or put at a disadvantage by leathers that are unlevel, over-long or too short.

• Before moving off, get settled, and quickly recheck the girth and make any further adjustments to the leathers. If riding a horse that is likely to be fresh, ride a hole or two shorter than you would do normally for security and balance, until you are both settled together.

• If the horse fidgets or moves off the moment you are in the saddle, do not tense through your back, or clamp your legs on to his sides or snatch at the rein contact, as this is likely to make things worse. Relax and quietly ask him to stand again; if he won't, move quietly off in walk – whatever you do, don't make an issue of it.

• Spend some time in walk; if you are in a school, you could ride turns, circles, changes of rein and also ask for some transitions to halt. This will help you get to know the length of the horse's stride, discover how responsive he is to hand and leg aids, and how supple he is. When you are happy that you can calmly start, stop and turn when you want to, only then begin to work in trot, and then in canter.

❺ Do not rush matters or resort to aggressive riding tactics

Not only is the horse an unknown quantity to you, but you are to him as well, so it may take a little while to 'gel' with each other. Don't allow anyone to pressure you into attempting anything you don't feel happy about doing, or to hurry you into each stage of the 'getting to know you' process before you feel ready for it.

❻ If you are trying out a horse to buy or loan ask the owner to ride it first

If you are a novice, ask your instructor to accompany you to give an opinion on its suitability for you. You should also insist that you try it out yourself in a safe, enclosed area.

The Causes of Problem Behaviour

Some forms of problem behaviour (such as rearing) can be dangerous for both horse and handler/rider – and to others who may be present. There is always a risk that undesirable behaviour will develop into an established habit, and will be repeated on future occasions unless action is taken to prevent this happening.

Solving any problem requires that the root cause is dealt with, not merely the symptoms. Using a different noseband may, for example, stop a horse from opening his mouth to evade the action of the bit, but if this behaviour stems from pain caused by sharp teeth or a heavy-handed rider, it will only prove to be a temporary remedy at best, and eventually the horse will resort to some other, possibly worse tactic.

Often there may be not just one, but several contributory factors, not all of which may appear immediately obvious. Some problem behaviours are also more easily remedied than others, and in some cases it may be necessary to seek expert professional or specialist help.

Rogue horses do exist, but often undesirable behaviours arise not because the horse is being awkward, but because he is unable to cope with the situation he finds himself in. If you react inappropriately, or punish him unfairly on such occasions, he will just become more confused, resentful, frightened and defensive, and the potential for an accident to arise increases.

When investigating the possible causes of problem behaviour, it is necessary to look at all areas of the horse's management.

❶ Has the horse's routine changed?
Has be been moved to a new yard, been given new field or stable companions, or even changed stables within the same yard: all of these can cause acute anxiety for some equines.

❷ Has the horse been over-confined?
Over-confinement within a stable can also encourage a number of behavioural and riding problems. Stabling may be necessary at certain times of the year, but try to ensure as much time as possible each day is spent out in the field grazing with other horses.

❸ Review the horse's diet
Work out a diet appropriate to age, weight, temperament and exercise. More owners are guilty of overfeeding than underfeeding. Inappropriate diet can promote problem behaviour; for instance, a horse on a low-forage, high-concentrate ration may spend too little time eating and become bored, leading to the development of stable vices.

❹ Assess whether the horse is in pain or suffering from a physical problem
- Pain, or some other physical problem (for example, poor eyesight).
- Poor shoeing.
- Incorrectly fitting, or unsuitable saddlery and bitting.
- Old injuries that appear to have healed, but which may cause ongoing difficulties due to altered muscular development and mechanical restrictions in the way the limb(s) move.
- Roughness on the part of the rider/handler.

❺ Is the horse unwilling or *unable* to do what is asked of it?
- Has it had a lack of education?
- Has there been a lack of clear communication on the part of the rider/handler?
- Is the horse physically unable to do what is asked of it? Is the work excessively taxing, of a nature not suited to the horse's temperament and abilities, or has constant mental as well as physical pressure been placed on it to improve?
- Has a previous accident or incident resulted in the horse being frightened or injured? Equines will very often remember such experiences.

Getting Help

If you experience a problem with your horse, whether it is when handling or riding him, don't battle on alone – seek help before the situation gets further out of hand and possibly dangerous. The longer you leave things, the more established the problem will become, making it harder to remedy; and inevitably this will undermine your confidence, leaving you even less able to cope safely.

❶ Seek professional help and advice

Although other owners will often be only too eager to offer advice, it is usually best to seek professional help. Many problems have their origins in physical discomfort, and although low-grade pain is not always immediately obvious to a less experienced eye, even at a minor level it can frequently be a source of difficulty. It is therefore always a good idea to eliminate this as a possible cause of bad behaviour by asking your vet to check the horse over, and a reputable saddle fitter look at your tack. Sometimes removing the discomfort may remedy the problem; although often the anticipation of pain remains for some time, or behavioural patterns have become so established that further work in handling or schooling is needed.

❷ Use the services of an instructor

A good (and insured) instructor can be a useful starting point in helping you, and having assessed the nature of the problem, should be able to either help you with it, or point you in the direction of someone who can. Do make a few enquiries as to his/her background first; you don't necessarily need the most highly-qualified person. Someone newly trained may lack the ability and depth of experience you need, whilst another person with the same qualifications may have been teaching for years and therefore have a huge fund of knowledge, but just never continued to take further exams. If it is recommended that the horse receives remedial schooling, it is also important to take lessons immediately following on from this, if difficulties are not to re-occur.

❸ Recognize that long-standing problems will not be cured overnight

Some problems may take much time, patience, and often money to effect a remedy. Some 'cures' may not be permanent, and the horse is likely to revert in times of stress; others may be incurable, in which case you will need to think seriously about the horse's future. An animal that displays potentially dangerous behaviour should not be passed on to anyone else, and although it may be a difficult decision to make, the best course of action in such circumstances is probably to have him euthanased, both for the sake of the animal as well as for the safety of the people he comes in contact with.

COMPLEMENTARY MEDICINE

Holistic medicine to treat both physical and behavioural problems is becoming increasingly popular, and in many instances has proved successful. Avoid attempting DIY remedies, as it is easy to go astray; if you wish to explore this approach, contact a vet who specializes in holistic veterinary treatment, or ask them to refer you to a qualified practitioner. No reputable practitioner will treat your horse without veterinary referral anyway, and you should beware of those who do not observe this.

INDEX

Page numbers in **bold** refer to substantial treatment of subject
Page numbers in *italic* refer to illlustrations